Radical **Prayers**

on Peace, Love, and Nonviolence

John Dear

Pace e Bene Press

Radical Prayers by John Dear

Published by Pace e Bene Press

To order individual copies or bulk copies,
visit: www.paceebene.org, email: info@paceebene.org, call 510-268-8765.

Author's Website: www.johndear.org

Library of Congress Cataloging-in-Publication Data
Dear, John 1959-
Radical Prayers / John Dear
ISBN-13: 978-0-9978337-1-3
ISBN-10: 0-9978337-1-8

Library of Congress Control Number: 2017917844

Cover artwork by: Sandy Vaillancourt
© 2017 Sandy Vaillancourt. Used with permission.
www.sandyvallaincourt.com
Cover design and layout: Ryan Hall
Interior design and layout: Erin Bechtol

Contents

For Mairead Maguire,
Friend and Peacemaker

Introduction

Reflections on Prayer and Nonviolence

Prayer and nonviolence go hand in hand.

On the one hand, prayer is a daily journey toward ever-deepening intimacy with the God of peace in the Holy Spirit of peace. Through daily quiet meditation, the God of peace we encounter in our prayer disarms us, heals us and strengthens us to go forth and make peace, practice nonviolence, and love others.

True prayer never leads to violence. It does not make us more violent, more warlike, or more militaristic. It does not bear the bad fruit of violence, hatred, or war. It does invite us to look deeply within, and sheds light on our shadow side. It opens a space for God to draw closer, shine God's healing light within us, and share God's peace with us, and so makes us more peaceful, more loving, more nonviolent. Even as we struggle with our weaknesses, problems, and violence, daily prayerful meditation keeps us on an even keel, going forward in nonviolence, and helping us to become better, more peaceful peacemakers.

On the other hand, nonviolence is not possible without regular, prayerful meditation. The practice of active nonviolence drives us to our knees. It turns us to God and regular, devout prayer. The life of active nonviolence requires one to renounce violence and weapons, head out into the world of war with a message of peace, and places one's entire security in the God of peace alone.

If you are nonviolent, you need God. You have to pray all the time; God is the higher power you rely on.

If you are violent, you don't need God. You have your guns, weapons, and money to rely on, and so you do not pray and your faith withers and your selfishness, greed, and violence increase. In the end, your own violence and your refusal to take time with the God of peace do not help you. When trouble comes, instead of leaning on God, you can fall apart or resort to violence and make matters far worse.

Nonviolent people turn to God in prayer throughout the day for protection, security, blessings, and fecundity. That is the Christian way, the human ideal. That is the path of the peacemaker.

Prayer and nonviolence are best learned through actual experience. People like me can write and lecture all day long, but it finally comes down to you, the individual, choosing to pray, choosing to practice nonviolence, choosing to connect prayer with nonviolence, and actively pursuing the life of peace and the God of peace.

One learns to pray by praying. One becomes more nonviolent by consciously trying to be nonviolent, renouncing violence, and engaging in active love and truth for global justice and disarmament every minute, every hour, every day of one's life.

Prayer is about a relationship. It is about your relationship with God. As in any healthy, loving relationship, we want to spend quality time with the one we love and care for, in loving attention, being fully present to the other, sharing our deepest thoughts, hopes, and concerns with one another, and listening carefully to the other.

In a healthy loving relationship, one person speaks and the other listens attentively. Then after a while, the other person speaks and the first person listens attentively. Eventually, the two enter into silent, loving adoration. This gentle, loving, nonviolent communication can go on for eternity.

That's what prayerful meditation is all about. It's our gentle, loving, nonviolent communication with the God of peace and love, our intimate communion with God. It involves sharing our deepest thoughts, hopes, and concerns with the God of peace who loves us, and noticing how God listens to us, loves us, and cares for us. It's also about our being quiet in the presence of God, and trying to listen attentively to the voice of God in silence, love, and stillness as God whispers to us, touches us, and speaks to our hearts. Eventually, it's about entering into silent, intimate, loving adoration of your God.

This takes us way beyond any kind of religious obligation. If we look at prayer as our quality time with the One who loves us infinitely, then prayer, or silent meditation, is something we will seek every chance we can.

Prayer is the gentle, loving, intimate communion and dialogue between two beings who love one another—ourselves and God. But this prayer of peace and love then leads us to widen our loving communion with God into universal communion with all humanity and all creation. In a world of total violence, injustice, and war, prayer rooted in true nonviolence naturally leads to public work for peace and universal nonviolent love.

If we want to respect God and deepen our intimate relationship with God, then we need to take quality time with God every day. Silent, prayerful meditation can become a daily ritual, a formal check-in time, when we show up for God. Over time, God is so happy that we show up that God shows up too, and we sit together in peace and get to know one another.

I recommend spending thirty minutes in silent meditation every day, preferably in the morning. Pick a private, peaceful space, sit alone, in solitude, open your heart to God and focus your attention on the God of peace. Our quiet prayer time with God, our daily silent meditation, becomes part of our normal, ordinary routine, just like brushing our teeth, taking a shower, doing the dishes, and attending to our day-to-day errands. During this time, we talk to God, listen to God, receive God's healing peace, and adore God. This process continually heals us, disarms us, guides us, and prepares us to go forth into the world of violence in God's spirit of creative, disarming nonviolence. It helps to write down afterwards reflections on your encounter with God, so that you remember them.

There are a million reasons not to take quality time for daily meditation. We are busy people! But wisdom suggests that making meditation a priority in our lives transforms us for the better, and helps us as we seek justice and disarmament in the world.

Daily meditation helps us rise above the world's horrors and give us a glimpse of the big picture—of God's reign of peace and God's long-haul view of things. In doing so, it can help lift us out of despair, anger, depression, and fear, and instill a bottom line of hope that only God's spirit can bring. Daily meditation keeps us focused on the truth of life, our relationship with God, our desire to be loving, nonviolent people, and the upcoming event of our deaths. It prepares us for that great day when we are welcomed home by God to dwell in the house of God forever. By taking time each day for peaceful meditation, we practice for that day, and gain a bedrock of faith, love, and trust that will, hopefully, ease us through the great transition into eternal life.

Ultimately, daily prayerful meditation reminds us of our basic identities—that we are first and foremost sons and daughters of the God of peace, called to live in God's peace and be peacemakers in a world of violence and war.

By returning to the God of peace in our prayer time, we reclaim the basic core of our identities and find new strength to go forward on the road to peace.

That's why I think daily meditation is politically dangerous and a threat to the culture of violence and war. As we combine prayer and nonviolence we step into a new kind of dangerous mysticism where we lose our allegiance to the nation/state, and become full time citizens of God's reign; where we give up our idolatry of money, power, and weapons, and trust solely in God; where we put down the sword and let go of violence, and take up the cross and walk the way of nonviolence; where we dare reach out in universal love to sisters and brothers across the planet, even those declared enemies of the state. This daily disarmament of the heart transforms us. Through our ongoing disarmament, the world is a little bit more disarmed.

We've been taught by the culture of war that God blesses America, defends us in war, wants us to be rich, and crushes our enemies. The Gospel, on the other hand, teaches us that God is a God of love, a God of peace, a God of nonviolence. The scandal of God is God's total nonviolence and God's desire that humanity turn to total nonviolence. As people of faith and prayer, we try to pursue Jesus' teachings on nonviolence, enter into the liminal space of the nonviolence of God, let God's nonviolence disarm us and transform us, and follow Jesus courageously as public peacemakers on the way of the cross toward a new culture of nonviolence.

As peacemakers, we are trying to live daily the peace we experience in the presence of God during our regular quiet meditation. We go forth in that spirit of healing peace and nonviolence to love and serve God and humanity. As we experience God as a God of peace, love, and nonviolence, we try to be God's people of peace, love, and nonviolence. We fail time and time again, so we go back to our daily encounter in prayerful meditation, and recommit ourselves all over again to God and God's mission for justice and peace. We go forth and try to live, teach, and promote nonviolence as a way of life and a vision for the world, that we might all pursue a new culture of nonviolence.

The practice of private prayerful meditation and active public peacemaking is God's will for us. God wants to use us as peacemakers in God's plan for the coming of justice and peace on earth. Our daily prayer and meditation prepares us for this holy mission. Because of our bedrock relationship with God in our regular prayer, we can handle any outcome. We can face rejection, betrayal, suffering, and death, just as Jesus did, in a spirit of peace, love, and nonviolence. As we go forward in our work for peace and nonviolence, we lean on God, dwell in God's peace, and trust God, come what may. We can do this because we have spent our lives one day at a time sitting with God, getting to know God, letting God love us, and living out God's spirit of peace and love.

Actually, there are many ways to pray—probably as many ways to pray as there are people. I've been describing here the daily practice of silent meditation, where we sit in solitude, enter God's presence, and give God our full attention. Other traditional forms of prayer include *lectio divina* (reading the scriptures slowly with devotion every day); chanting (singing devotional hymns over and over again); communal prayer (where we gather together in small circles for prayer, whether over a meal or for specific help); and Eucharistic prayer (in the Mass, when we hear the scriptures and share the bread and cup). Sometimes, when we can't pray, we can recite simple repetitive mantras like the Rosary or the Jesus prayer ("Lord Jesus Christ, son of the living God, have mercy on me a sinner") over and over again. They help ground us in God and strengthen our faith.

Another basic form of prayer is intentional, intercessory prayer, when we ask God directly for what we need. That is what this book is about. I recommend we take formal silent meditation time every day, but I also recommend that throughout our day, we intentionally ask God for what we need, and for the needs of all our sisters and brothers, all the creatures, and Mother Earth herself.

In this little book I offer the prayers we rarely hear spoken out loud—prayers for an end to racism, sexism, greed, poverty, war, gun violence, executions, nuclear weapons, and environmental destruction; prayers also for the coming of God's reign of peace, for blessings on the grassroots movements of nonviolence, for a new culture of nonviolence. These prayers lead to the ultimate last prayer—a heartfelt prayer for humanity's conversion to total nonviolence, which I believe is the ultimate prayer, the prayer of Jesus—"your kingdom of nonviolence come, your will of nonviolence be done."

This book is best read a few pages at a time, not all at once. I hope it will help us to pray for humanity and creation, in our own words. It is a book to keep by your bedside, one you can turn to before you go to sleep or upon waking up. It could be kept in your place of daily meditation, so that at the beginning or end of your quiet time with God, you can quietly recite one of these prayers of peace, love, and nonviolence.

They may sound like "radical prayers," but actually they are simple, ordinary prayers of the heart, prayers for universal peace in a time of permanent war, prayers for universal love in a time of increasing hate, prayers of total nonviolence in a time of widespread, systemic violence.

I'd like to thank my Pace e Bene colleagues for help with this project—Ryan Hall, Ken Butigan, Veronica Pelicaric, and Kit Evans Ford. I also thank Connie Clark for proofreading the manuscript, Erin Bechtol for designing the layout, and Sandy Vaillancourt for her beautiful artwork.

May the God of peace hear our prayers, turn us into people of Gospel nonviolence, and strengthen us to go forward in a campaign of public nonviolence to work for an end to war, poverty, racism, nuclear weapons, and environmental destruction, and for the coming of a new culture of peace and nonviolence. May they inspire you to pursue your intimate relationship with your beloved God, that you might become a friend of God, that you might listen to God, and that you might go forth to do God's work of peace, love, and nonviolence.

Amen.

—John Dear
Labor Day, 2017

Part One:

Thanks, Praise, and Adoration

God of peace, how awesome is your name
through all the earth.
You have set your majesty above the heavens. . . .
I will praise you, God of peace, with all my heart;
I will declare all your wondrous deeds.
I will delight and rejoice in You;
I will sing hymns to your name, Most High.

–Psalm 8:2; 9:2-3

You Are Unconditional, Universal Nonviolence

Dear God,

Thank you so much
for loving me
and every human being.
Thank you for creating us
and this beautiful world
to live in peace
with you and each other.

You are unconditional, universal love.
You are unconditional, universal peace.
You are unconditional, universal nonviolence.
You are so loving,
peaceful,
and nonviolent
that you give us the freedom
to choose violence,
to reject you and one another,
to hurt ourselves and the whole world.

You try through your spirit of nonviolent love
to help us,
disarm us,
heal us,
and lead us again down your path of eternal peace.
You never give up on us.

I am amazed
at your unconditional,
nonviolent,
universal,
suffering love.
In this love, you hold me
and every human being
with infinite kindness and gentleness.
You long to welcome each one of us home

to dwell in your peace forever.
Thank you for this astounding suffering love.

For such love,
such gentleness,
such steadfast nonviolence,
I adore you
and praise you
and bless you.
I worship you now and forever
as the one true God,
the God of peace and universal love,
the God of universal nonviolence
who, in the end, will win out.

One day, you will disarm us all,
and lead us all to your home
of eternal peace.

Thank you, beloved God.
I give thanks to you from this moment on,
and for the rest of eternity.

Amen.

Thank You for Being with Me on My Journey

Dear God,

Thank you for creating me,
for giving me life,
for giving me my body,
for placing me in the world,
in these particular circumstances,
for so many blessings,
for calling me to live life to the fullest
and to walk the path of life in peace with you.

Thank you for being with me on my journey,
with all its ups and downs,
all its mountains and valleys.

Thank you for family,
friends, communities,
education, health, food,
housing, and dignity.

Thank you for the kindness of others,
for the support of loved ones,
for the beauty of creation,
for the road to peace.

Thank you for letting me see your beautiful creation—
the oceans and mountains,
the deserts and forests,
the sky and the canyons.

Thank you for letting me enjoy so many creatures—
the dogs, cats, horses, elephants, coyotes,
bobcats, snakes, hawks, owls, ravens, sparrows,
blue jays, dolphins, and whales.

You have been with me every step of my journey.
You have never left me.

I have left you,
over and over again,
but you kept coming back,
calling me to your side.
You sought me out and watched over me
with your unconditional love.

You have only shown compassion,
mercy and love to me.
You were never mean, never violent.
You never threatened me, never hurt me.

You have encouraged me every step of the way.
When I took the time to listen,
I heard your encouraging words.
I knew you were there.
You have taken care of me.
You have been my protector,
my shield, my rock, my refuge.

Thank you for accompanying me
on my journey through life.
I love you forever because of that.
And I ask you to stay with me
until that moment
when I see you face to face.

Until then, guide me, help me,
protect me, and bless me.
Show me how to best serve you
and my sisters and brothers,
and be my faithful companion
and dear friend
from now on.

Amen.

May I Always Be Surrendered to You

Dear God,

More than anything,
I want to surrender myself to you.
I know now that you are the God
of infinite love,
peace, and compassion.

Even if no one else believes in you,
even if the churches support the culture's violence
and preach a false god of violence,
I want to serve you and belong to you,
God of peace,
and love you all my days.
I throw my lot in with you,
and offer myself to you.

But even as I desire to give myself
in full surrender to you,
I do not do it,
and I cannot, for I am limited,
broken,
wounded, and blind.

And so I ask you:
take me to yourself.
You want me to give myself freely to you,
and I want to give myself freely to you,
and so I ask you to take me,
body and soul,
mind and heart,
to yourself.
I am all yours.
Do with me what you will.
I give you permission to take me
and use me as you will from now on.

I belong to you.
My body, my soul, my mind, my heart—
they are yours.
I give them freely to you.
You own them, I do not.
Let them be of loving service to you from now on.
Let me not be surrendered to the culture,
its violence,
its hatred,
fear,
darkness,
and despair.

Guide me that I may give myself to you
every day from now on,
in peace, hope, and love.
Let me trust in you,
that I may always be there for you,
with you.
You are always there for me;
give me the grace to be wholeheartedly there for you.

I surrender myself to you.
May I always be surrendered to you.
At the moment of my death,
may I surrender to you in peace and gratitude.
May that final surrender be gentle and peaceful.
With every breath,
until my last breath,
let my spirit say with the dying Jesus,
"Into your hands I commend my spirit."

Amen.

You Are Wildly in Love with Me and Everyone

Dear God,

What were you thinking when you created us,
when you loved us into being,
when you gave us this paradise,
knowing full well we would reject you,
reject one another,
and reject paradise?
Didn't you see that you had thousands of years
of suffering ahead of you,
that you would have to watch us hurt one another,
kill one another,
and destroy your creation?

Ah, so that's what makes you God!
You have infinite suffering love,
a nonviolent love that gives us
the freedom to reject you and one another,
a nonviolent love that still reaches out to help us,
a nonviolent love that forgives a billion times over,
forgets the past,
and sees a new future of universal love
in an eternal moment of peace.

So you really are the perfect parent.
Like a gentle father,
like a tender, loving mother,
you feed us,
hold us when we cry,
help us take our first step,
encourage us to walk,
show us creation,
wipe away our tears,
make us laugh,
and spend all your time with us
in loving concern.
You can't get enough of us.

You are wildly in love with me and everyone,
all one hundred billion people who ever lived.
You want to spend eternity with each one of us,
listen to us forever,
smile at us,
love us,
dote over us,
guide us,
help us,
and watch us grow up.

You want to share your paradise with us.
You want us to be yours,
to be your beloved sons and daughters
who tend your vineyard
and enjoy an eternal banquet with you.

Count me in.
Though I make mistakes,
complain too much,
cry out loud,
walk away from you
and hurt others,
be my loving mother, my gentle father.

Help me to become the beloved child
you created me to be,
to live and act like you,
in compassionate nonviolent love,
that I may live in the fullness of peace
with you and everyone,
now and forever.

Amen.

With You, There Is Meaning, There Is Love, There Is Peace

Dear God,

You are Mount Everest.
You are the Pacific Ocean.
You are the Grand Canyon.
You are the big blue sky of the high desert.
You are the dark night of ten thousand stars.
You are the sun and the moon
and the clouds and the rain
and the snow and the wind.
You are always there.
You are so faithful,
so steady,
so big,
so small,
so calm.
You are the center of stillness.
You have always been and always will be.

Perhaps that is why we reject you,
because instead of mindful stillness
we prefer to run around in mindless chaos.
We don't know any better.
We are like wild animals who have yet to be tamed.
We let our minds zigzag
from one crazy thought to the next,
and let our lives drift
from current to current.
We feed ourselves on the mindlessness of the culture,
from the endless TV noise
to the voices of exclusivity
to the violence and hostility that surrounds us.

We think of anything and everything under the sun,
everything but you and your peace.

We give in to the narrow-mindedness
of nationalism and privilege
and fail to see the big picture.
We refuse to step into the big space of your stillness.
We find it boring.
We prefer the chaos of our violence.
And so we know nothing of your stillness,
your peaceableness,
your gentleness.

Still, there you are, inviting us into your stillness,
your peace,
the present moment,
the fullness of life.
You are the present moment.
You are peace.
You are life itself.
With you, there is nothing boring.
Everything pales in comparison to you.
Your presence, your peace, your stillness
are infinitely interesting and healing.

With you, there is meaning,
there is love,
there is peace.

Help us to step into your presence
and live in your present moment of peace,
that we might be present to ourselves and one another,
and one day learn from you the wisdom of peace.

Amen.

You Never Give Up on Us

Dear God,

You could wipe us out in the blink of an eye
if you wanted to.
You could send an asteroid,
let us blow up our nuclear weapons,
let loose catastrophic climate change.
Any one of us would do that if we had experienced
the rejection we have shown you.

But you do not do that.
You never would.
You couldn't.
You remain loving,
gentle,
and nonviolent,
no matter what.

We, on the other hand,
want to wipe ourselves out in the blink of an eye.
We do not want to wait for an asteroid to hit.
We eagerly build more nuclear weapons,
hasten catastrophic climate change,
kill one another,
let millions starve,
decimate a multitude of species,
and destroy the earth.
We reject you, and so we reject ourselves
and one another
and creation.

But you do not reject us.
You keep after us.
You keep nudging us
with your encouraging nonviolent love
to become who we were created to be,
instruments of your nonviolent love.

You want us to show nonviolent love to ourselves,
to one another, to all the creatures, and to creation itself.
And you help us do that.

You send us saints and peacemakers
to show us the way.
You open up new ways for us to accept
ourselves and one another in peace.
You keep giving us a second chance,
and a third, and a fourth, and a thousandth.
You never give up on us.

We give up on you over and over again,
a thousand times a day,
but you never give up on us.

You are a big God, the Almighty,
and you consciously choose to reject
violence and destruction.
You come to us in the still, small breeze,
in the present moment of peace,
in the quiet, running stream,
in the song of the bird,
in the warmth of the sun,
in the kindness of another.
You insist on peace, hope, and love.
That is who you are.

Let it be that way for each one of us, too.
Make us as nonviolent,
as compassionate, as loving,
as peaceful as you.

Amen.

You Look at Us Through the Eyes of Compassion

Dear God,

Someone once said to me,

"I know why I'm going to heaven—
because I'm so compassionate!"

But that is not true for any one of us.

The reason you will welcome us into heaven
is because you are so compassionate!

Yes, you show compassion to us
in our frailty, our brokenness, our vulnerability,
our helplessness and poverty of spirit.
You know our needs.
You know our sins and darkness and shadow side.
You know how we hurt ourselves and others.
You know how,
even when we try to show compassion to some,
we still withhold compassion from others
and that we stray far from your boundless compassion.

Sooner or later, we will all suffer and die.
In our pain, illness, and death
you show the most compassion for us.
You take pity on us,
even as we refuse to take pity on others,
especially the poor, the homeless,
the hungry, the imprisoned, the dying.

You look at each one of us
through the eyes of compassion
and reach out to help us, strengthen us,
and lead us into the fullness of life.

As we grow in awareness of your compassion,

give us new strength to show
more compassion to others,
especially the marginalized, suffering, and dying.

Thank you for showing compassion to us.

Help us to show compassion to one another,
to create more compassionate societies,
to welcome a new world of compassion.

Inspire us to discover our common humanity
with new compassion for every human being,
every creature, and creation itself.
Strengthen us that we might reflect your compassion
toward everyone we meet.

May we always give thanks to you
for your great compassion
and share this gift of compassion
with everyone everywhere from now on.

Amen.

Part Two:

For Myself

Who may dwell on your holy mountain?
Whoever walks without blame,
doing what is right,
speaking truth from the heart;
who does not slander a neighbor,
does no harm to another,
and never defames a friend.

–Psalm 15:1-3

Let Eternal Life in Your Peaceful Presence Begin Today

Dear God,

I want to live in loving relationship with you.
I think that is what you want from me and everyone,
but I don't know how to do it.
Please help me.

Give me the grace to show up each day
in quiet time with you,
to take the time to be with you,
to be fully present,
open,
attentive,
listening,
and loving,
that I may walk through the days of my life with you.

I know you always want to be with me,
even when your presence feels like absence.
I know you are a doting father, a loving mother,
who wants to attend to your beloved child,
to every human being.
Thank you for wanting to be close to me,
for loving me
and wanting to love me
and wanting to spend time with me.

But I forget.
I forget to take time with you.
I get busy,
stuck in a rut,
overwhelmed by my day-to-day tasks.
Even when I do sit down in quiet time,
I let my mind wander and I start thinking
about all I have to do this day.

But that is not what I want.
My deepest desire is to sit with you
in intimate love and quiet adoration.
I want to be your beloved,
your friend,
your child.
I want you to find a home in me, too.
I want you to be my rock,
my stronghold,
my fortress,
my safety,
my inner paradise.

And I want to share my life with you,
to spend my life in love with you,
so that when I die,
I already know you,
and you already know me,
and I can enjoy eternity in your presence.
Indeed, let eternal life in your peaceful presence
begin today,
right now, this very moment,
and help me to live every day
as if I was already in the fullness of eternal life.

Give me the grace to be with you every day.
Open my heart and ears and eyes to feel your presence,
see you around me, and hear your word.
Feel free to speak to me and share your life with me.
Help me to live with you
as I would with an intimate friend,
that I might always be present to you,
ready to hear you, open to your guidance,
as you are already always present to me.

Thank you.
Amen.

Restore My Spirit, Fill Me with Your Peace

Dear God,

I am broken,
bruised,
sad,
lonely,
and depressed.
Please come and comfort me
with your abiding presence and kindness.
Restore my spirit,
fill me with your peace,
and help me to be a source
of peace and kindness for others.

I have tried to be an instrument of peace,
and just as Jesus promised,
I have been hurt and rejected.
People have told me off and walked away.
I have tried to respond nonviolently,
but I often fail.

My wound is great.
I've been hurt by violent people throughout my life,
from my relatives,
classmates,
and neighbors,
to the police,
military,
and church officials.
I've often internalized that violence,
turned against myself,
and nurtured a lifelong anger and resentment.
And so the wound festers.

Heal me, God of compassion.
Help me to let go of those feelings of violence,

to accept myself,
hold my inner child,
befriend myself,
and show mercy to myself.
Send your spirit upon me
that I may show kindness to myself,
just as you show kindness to me.
Let me model the healing that I seek
for all others and creation.

Lift my spirit,
that I may feel your loving presence
and know that you are always with me.
Touch my wounds and heal them,
that I may not hurt or wound anyone,
that I might be your wounded healer,
a source of compassion and nonviolent love for others.

Help me to forgive those who have hurt me,
to let go of anger and resentment
and to lift the spirits of those who are sad and hurt,
that together we might try
to heal one another
and creation itself.

Amen.

Help Me to Be Nonviolent to Myself and to Make Peace with Myself

Dear God,

Help me to be nonviolent to myself.
Give me the grace to treat myself nonviolently
so that your love and grace might dwell within me
and I might radiate your peace for the rest of my life.

Even if I don't want to be nonviolent to myself,
even if I continue the old patterns
of self-hatred and low self-esteem,
help me to be nonviolent to myself.
Do it for your sake.
Help me to be gentle with myself for your sake.

You love me.
There are large parts of myself that I do not love,
but give me the grace to love myself
because you love me as I am.
Help me to love myself and be nonviolent to myself
as a way for me to show my love for you.

In the light of your love,
I let go of self-hatred and low self-esteem.
I let go of the violence that lingers within me,
the hostility toward myself,
the inner rage and anger that boils just under the surface.
Help me to walk in your presence,
to feel your love,
that my inner violence will dissipate,
that I might begin to make peace with myself
and feel good about myself.

Jesus taught us to love our neighbors as ourselves.
If I don't love myself,
I won't be able to love anyone else.

I want to love everyone.
So help me then to love myself as you love me.
Help me to be kind and merciful to myself.
Then I will be kind and merciful to others.
Inspire me to give myself a break,
to let myself off the hook,
to show unconditional friendliness to myself.
Teach me to cultivate inner peace,
inner nonviolence and gentleness,
that I may dwell in your peace,
and radiate your peace to others.

With you by my side,
teach me to accept myself and love myself
so that I may discover a new healthy self-esteem,
that I may respect myself and reclaim my inner dignity.

Through this inner transformation,
help me to love and respect others,
to treat everyone with dignity
as I treat myself with love and dignity.

Thank you.
Amen.

Do Not Be Afraid. Live in My Love, Receive My Peace, Walk in My Light.

Dear God,

Jesus instructed his disciples
over and over again
not to be afraid.
I would like to obey Jesus and not live in fear,
so give me the grace of fearlessness.

Help me not to be afraid of others,
not to be afraid to be alone,
not to be afraid of life or afraid of death.
Instead, let me live in your love and peace,
and trust that you are by my side,
that I need not fear,
that you are there to protect me.

Be my security,
that I need not resort to violence
or weapons or greed or power,
that I can make peace with everyone,
that I can radiate and share your peace with the world
because I dwell in your peaceful presence.

So many voices in the culture tell us to be afraid.
We let those voices seep in,
and start to fear anyone who is different from us.
Such fear is useless and harmful.
It only makes us unhappy and inspires violence.
It leads us to terror and war.

Help me to hear the voice of Jesus as he says:
"Do not be afraid.
You are my beloved.
Live in my love,

receive my peace,
walk in my light."

Show me your abiding presence
in the small moments of my day
that I may learn to feel your loving presence
and walk in your peace.

Your love overcomes fear.
Your love evaporates fear.
If I dwell in your peaceful love,
I need not fear anyone or anything.
I don't even have to fear death.
In your loving presence,
I know that my survival is guaranteed,
that I will always dwell in your loving, peaceful presence,
that with you,
there is nothing to fear.

From now on,
I will not fear anyone or anything.
I will walk in your love and peace,
and spread your love and peace everywhere I go.
Give me the grace to live fearlessly,
in the spirit of your peace,
love, and nonviolence,
that I might learn to trust you.

Thank you.
Amen.

Keep Me from Getting Stuck in the Rut of Hatred, Anger, and Resentment

Dear God,

Save me from the hard emotions—
hatred,
anger,
and resentment.
Teach me to let go of these hard feelings,
not to get stuck in them,
and to live instead in the wisdom of your love,
compassion, and nonviolence.

When someone hurts me,
help me not to give in to hatred.
Help me to recognize the deep wounds,
shame, and humiliation that lie below their surface,
that I might discover your compassion for them,
that I might forgive them for hurting me,
and drop any feelings of hatred.

Hatred is like poison:
it only leads to death.
Teach me over time to feel compassion for everyone,
even those who have hurt me over the course of my life.
Remind me to bring them to you in prayer,
to discover your compassion for them and for me,
to forgive them as a daily practice.
Keep me from getting stuck in the rut of hatred.
Let me dwell in your love and light.
In this way, heal me and heal everyone.

Don't let me give in to anger, either.
Anger is just the sign that I've been deeply hurt,
and it easily leads to retaliation and violence.
Jesus taught us not to get angry,
but to show love, forgiveness, and compassion.

He urged us instead to apologize
and reconcile with those whom we have hurt.
He did not get angry as he was betrayed,
denied,
abandoned,
tortured,
and killed.
He responded nonviolently
with forgiveness and compassion.
He showed no anger
or desire for revenge
in his resurrection appearances.
Instead he radiated only peace and compassion.
Let it be the same with me.

Help me to let go of anger.
Cut the roots of my anger.
Heal my wounds that I may spend my life
not in anger but in compassion,
not in hatred but in love,
not in war but in peace.

Dear God,
dig deep inside me and root out all my resentments.
Heal those deep wounds that stretch back to my youth,
that have become entrenched like barnacles on my heart.
Scrape them away.
Help me to forgive everyone who has ever hurt me,
so that these resentments disappear.
Replace them with your love,
light, compassion, and peace.
Let peaceableness become my daily path.

Thank you for hearing my prayer.
Amen.

Come and Dwell Within Me from Now On

Dear God,

Come dwell in me.
You made me,
you love me,
you want to be with me—welcome!
Make yourself at home inside me.

I'm sorry, dear God,
for all the ways I have rejected you,
hurt you,
ignored you,
or brushed you aside.
I am inhospitable to you,
even though you have shown me
only loving kindness and compassion.

No more!
Come and dwell within me from now on.
I give you my heart, make it your home.
It belongs to you.
My heart,
my soul,
my body,
my spirit,
my mind,
my will—
I give them all to you.
Make them your home on earth,
that you may dwell within me,
that it might no longer be me who lives
but you who live in me,
who love others through me,
who make peace with humanity and creation through me.

You want this, and so do I.
But I am slow, dull, forgetful.
I can be cruel, mean, and unwelcoming.
I'm this way to myself and others,
and certainly to you.

Come dwell within me anyway!
I invite you to set up home in my heart,
to make it your dwelling place.
This is my deepest desire,
even if I do not say it often or show it to you.
Come, live inside me,
live with me,
let me feel your love and peace.

Dwell within me, dear God, from now on,
and I shall always dwell in your presence.
Then I shall radiate your love and peace,
do your will, and share your radiant peace wherever I go.
There could be no greater wish.

Thank you for hearing my prayer.
Amen.

Fashion My Heart After the Sacred Heart of the Nonviolent Jesus

Dear God,

Give me a nonviolent heart like yours.
Widen my heart to embrace every human being
as my sister and brother,
as you love every human being
a̶ ̶ ̶ ̶beloved daughter or son.

̶ ̶ ̶as grown cold.
̶ ̶ ̶rdened by years of selfishness and violence.
̶ ̶ck.
̶ ̶eal it, break it open,
̶ ̶r light shine through it.
̶ ̶king the way it should.

̶ ̶r fault, it's mine.
̶ ̶athy have set in.
̶ ̶feel empathy for others,
̶ ̶d their pain and brokenness,
̶ ̶npassion to them,
̶ ̶hat they do to me.

̶ ̶ch out in loving service of others.
̶ ̶are for those in need.
̶ ̶ork for justice and disarmament.
̶ ̶lf for others, as Jesus did,
̶ ̶will heal and widen.

̶ ̶servant of disarming love for others.
̶ ̶eart
̶ ̶o heal the broken-hearted.
̶ ̶y heart
̶ ̶our peace.

God does not desire the soul to undertake any labor, but only to take delight in the first fragrance of the flowers . . . the soul can obtain sufficient nourishment from its own garden.

St. Teresa

Transform my violent heart into your nonviolent heart,
that it might radiate your peace to one and all.

Fashion my heart after the sacred heart
of the nonviolent Jesus.
Give me a sacred heart, too,
that you might have a sacred place to dwell.

As you disarm my heart,
take it for yourself and share it with others.
I give it to you.
It's yours.
From now on,
my heart belongs to you.

Amen.

Give Me the Grace to Live the Life
of Gospel Nonviolence

Dear God,

Thank you for the gift of your love and your peace.
Give me the grace to live the life of Gospel nonviolence
that I might be a faithful follower of the nonviolent Jesus.
Send the Holy Spirit of nonviolence upon me
that I will love everyone,
from my neighbors to my enemies,
that I may see you in everyone,
and know everyone as my sister and brother,
and never hurt or fear anyone ever again.

Make me an instrument of your peace,
that I might give my life in the struggle
for justice and disarmament;
that I may work for the abolition of war,
poverty,
racism,
nuclear weapons,
and environmental destruction;
that I may always respond with love
and never retaliate with violence;
that I may accept suffering in the struggle for justice
and never inflict suffering or death on others;
that I may live more simply,
in solidarity with the world's poor,
that I may defend the poor and voiceless;
resist systemic injustice and institutionalized violence,
that I may help protect your creatures and creation,
that I may always choose life and resist the forces of death.

Guide me on the Way of nonviolence.

Help me to speak the truth of peace,
to practice boundless compassion,

to radiate unconditional love,
to forgive everyone who has ever hurt me,
to embody your nonviolence,
to walk with you in contemplative peace,
to be your beloved servant and friend.

Disarm my heart,
and I shall be your instrument
to disarm other hearts and the world.

Lead me, God of nonviolence,
with the whole human family,
into your nonviolent reign of justice and peace
where there is no more war,
no more injustice,
no more nuclear weapons,
and no more violence.
Make us the loving,
nonviolent,
peacemaking sons and daughters you created us to be.

I ask this in the name of the nonviolent Jesus,
our brother and our peace.

Amen.

Make Me a True Disciple of the Nonviolent Jesus

Dear God,

Help me to follow the nonviolent Jesus
all the days of my life.

Give me the grace to begin and end my day
in silent meditation with Jesus,
with regular reading of the Gospels,
with an awareness of his risen presence.
Help me to go through life
in his spirit and his peace.

Let me feel myself sent by him
to carry on his work of peace, love,
compassion, and nonviolence,
that I might heal the victims of violence,
denounce systemic injustice,
and announce the coming of your kingdom
of peace and nonviolence.

Give me the grace to take up the cross,
to walk the way of nonviolent resistance
into the culture of violence and injustice,
to respond with love and compassion
toward those who reject and hurt me and others.
Let my presence be healing,
peaceful,
disarming,
and loving,
so that people feel better from having been with me.
May they in fact feel your healing,
disarming spirit at work through me.

Let your Holy Spirit guide my choices and decisions,
that I may always serve others,
especially the poor and marginalized.

Make me a true disciple of the nonviolent Jesus,
that I might be his apostle of peace,
nonviolence, and compassion,
and help inspire a new generation of peacemakers.

Give me the grace at the hour of my death
to look back on my life with gratitude,
knowing that I tried to live every day
in the footsteps of the nonviolent Jesus.

May I surrender my life now and at that hour
into your hands and go home to you with confidence,
eager to hear your blessing,
"Well done, my good and faithful servant,
inherit the kingdom that was prepared for you
from the foundation of the world."

Thank you.
Amen.

Give Me the Grace to Live in Your Holy Present, Your Eternal Now

Dear God,

Help me to start living today as if
I were already in heaven,
as if eternity begins right this very minute.
In some ways, this is the most important prayer,
the prayer you want,
that we use our time wisely to get ready
to be in your company
by being fully, peacefully,
nonviolently in one another's company.

In heaven, I will see you as you are.
There, I will be fully healed,
filled with the peace and joy of your presence,
in unconditional nonviolent love
with all one hundred billion people who have ever lived.
I cannot comprehend that now,
in this mortal body,
I cannot comprehend that,
but prepare me now for that new day to come.

Let me live here in this body,
in this time and place,
as if I were in heaven,
already in eternity,
that I may feel your presence,
and know myself at home in your love and peace.

In that holy space, I will try to be nonviolent,
loving, and compassionate to those near and far.
I will speak out publicly against war,
injustice, and destruction,
and for justice and peace for the poor and creation.
Let me be your instrument

to inspire others to enter into your present moment
and practice your unconditional, nonviolent love
to everyone and all creation.

Thank you, Holy God,
for this holy present moment
of peace, love, and compassion.
Give me the grace to live in this holy moment,
your holy present,
your eternal now,
from now on.

Amen.

Part Three:

For All People

I will listen for the word of God;
surely the Lord will proclaim peace
to God's people, to the faithful,
to those who trust in God . . . .
Love and truth will meet;
Justice and peace will kiss.
Truth will spring from the earth;
Justice will look down from heaven.

−Psalm 85:9-12

Give Me a Heart as Wide as the World

Dear God,

Give me a heart as wide as the world
that I might love everyone as you do.
Open my heart to love every human being
as my sister and brother,
that I might practice your universal,
nonviolent love from now on.
Make me an instrument of your universal,
nonviolent love so that I become
the loving person you created me to be.

Most days, dear God, I do not feel like loving people.
I get mad at them, judge them, and condemn them.
I forget to see through the eyes of compassion,
and so I forget that they are my sisters and brothers.

Help me through my daily life
that I may see every human being as a sister or brother,
as someone you love,
that I may see them as you see them,
and love them as you love them.
I know this is possible because you have created us
to live according to your way
of unconditional, nonviolent love.
Open my heart to practice this way of universal,
unconditional, nonviolent love.

Help me to practice your way of loving nonviolence
toward everyone I know and meet,
that I might love my neighbor as myself,
and never hurt anyone ever again.
Your love melts away all indifference,
fear, worry, and violence.
If we live and walk in the way of your universal love,

we can never hurt anyone or sit idly by
while billions of people suffer hunger, war, and injustice.

Put universal love into action in me,
that I might reach out in love for others,
especially those most in need.
Give me a spirit of empathy
that I may feel for those who suffer
from oppression, injustice, and violence.
Give me a spirit of gentle activism
that I may work to relieve the suffering of others,
that my universal love may bear concrete good fruit
in the lives of the poor and needy.

Fix my heart that I may know
your unconditional love for me,
that I may radiate that same unconditional love
for every human being on earth, my sisters and brothers,
so that more and more, your universal love
will be the universal law,
and everyone will reject violence and injustice,
and learn to live in the peace that comes with your love.

Amen.

Give Me the Grace to Love the Enemies of My Nation

Dear God,

At the climax of his Sermon on the Mount,
Jesus commands us to "love your enemies . . .
that you may be sons and daughters
of the God who lets the sun rise on the good and the bad
and the rain to fall on the just and the unjust."

I know he's right, that loving the people
declared to be enemies by our nation
is the height of unconditional, universal love.
Please give me the grace to love the enemies of my nation.
Help us all to love our enemies.

God of peace and universal love,
I'm sick and tired of war, terrorism,
nuclear weapons, and the non-stop killings
that seem to be the norm.
Today our world wages permanent war
through terrorism, drones, corporate greed,
racism, the ongoing threat of nuclear destruction,
and environmental destruction.

Wake us up that we might end war
and killing once and for all
and institutionalize global, nonviolent love
so that we can welcome your gift of peace.

Few realize that they are sisters
and brothers of one another.
Few know that they are your beloved sons and daughters.
Help us to learn the truth about who we are,
about our fundamental identities,
that we might learn to love you and one another
and accept the astonishing social, economic, and political
implications of universal, nonviolent love.

Dear God, few people even know that you are
a God of universal, nonviolent love.
We don't think about the sun or the rain,
or about your lavish generosity,
whether or not we are worthy.
Few know that you are nonviolent,
that you treat everyone equally,
that you invite everyone into your universal,
nonviolent love.

Help us to learn.
Give us a new global vision.
Widen our hearts to embrace the whole human race.
Make us welcome the sunshine and rain with gratitude.

You are such a beautiful, loving God.
You love everyone, even those of us
who do not love you or one another.
You love even those of us
who would kill our sisters and brothers
and destroy your creation.
Love us all the way,
that we might grow in compassion,
peace, and justice, and become, for Jesus,
people of universal, nonviolent love.

Amen.

Help Us Abolish Racism and Sexism and See Everyone as a Sister and Brother

Dear God,

You are our compassionate father,
our loving mother,
our guiding spirit.
You enjoyed creating us in beautiful diversity.
Help us to welcome that diversity,
to celebrate human variety,
and to honor everyone in their lovely difference.

If we love everyone as they are
in all their beauty and diversity,
we catch a glimpse of you.

Thank you, God of peace,
for making us in all our beautiful diversity.
Help us to renounce prejudice and discrimination
and abolish racism that we might see everyone
as our beloved sisters and brothers.

Give the human family a new grace—
the grace of naming the stupidity
and ignorance of racism,
the wisdom to uphold the dignity and beauty
of every human being,
and the insight to see your beauty in one another,
especially those who are different.

You created us as men and women,
and gave us the gift of gender and sexuality.
Please help men to renounce and abolish sexism
once and for always,
that men might treat women as equals
everywhere around the world from now on,
that women might claim their dignity,

that men might become more nonviolent and humble
and women might be more empowered.

Give the human family a new grace—
the grace of living equality between the genders,
in every corner of the planet,
so that men and women might live around the world
as nonviolent brothers and sisters,
your beloved children,
as you intended us to live.

In our diversity, help us to accept everyone
with unconditional nonviolent love—
those of different religions,
different sexual orientations,
different nations,
different ages,
and different races.

Give the human family a new grace—
the grace of honoring every human being
as a beloved sister and brother,
that everyone might claim their dignity
as your beloved daughter and son,
that together we might welcome
your nonviolent reign of peace.

Amen.

May No Child Ever Suffer Hunger, Cruelty, Violence, or War Ever Again

Dear God,

Thank you for children,
for every little child in the world.
I pray for them all,
for a new miracle—
that no child will ever suffer hunger,
cruelty, indifference, violence,
murder, or war ever again.

Can I ask for that, God of peace?
Is that too much?
Isn't that your will?
Please inspire us to protect the children of the world,
that they not suffer hunger, disease,
violence, war, or cruelty,
that every child on the planet would be loved
unconditionally and nonviolently,
that a new generation of nonviolent children
grow up to become nonviolent adults
who transform the world into
a new place of nonviolence and peace.

God of peace,
please inspire parents not to harm their children,
not to hurt them,
not to strike them,
not to be violent to them.
Please give parents the grace
through a new global awareness and education
to practice unconditional love, tender compassion,
and creative nonviolence to their children.

Teach them nonviolent suffering love,
to love them even as they cry, scream, and kick,

so that their love will disarm and pacify their children,
and that love will take root in them
and give them a lifelong direction of nonviolent love.
Please disarm everyone so that no child or young adult
is ever sexually abused again.

Help us to create policies and societies
where children are revered, honored, and protected,
where the needs of every child are met,
where a climate of safety and nonviolence is created
so that children grow up in peace
and become the peacemakers you created them to be.

God of peace,
give every adult the new grace
to be nonviolent to children,
to educate children in your way of nonviolence,
and to work for a more nonviolent world
so that generations to come will live in peace
with one another and your creation.

You desire this, God of peace.
Inspire us to make it happen,
and in the process, share with us the joy
of children that we, too, might reclaim
our childlike wonder
and welcome your kingdom of love and peace
with sincere love, thanks, and joy.

Amen.

Please Create a Safe Haven of Nonviolence in Every Household in the World

Dear God,

I pray for all the families of the world,
that every family may grow
from a family of violence
to a family of nonviolence.

Please end the violence in every house in the world.
Please create a safe haven of nonviolence
in every household in the world.

Help parents to be as nonviolent as possible
to each other and to each child.
Inspire them to affirm and love each child,
and never to strike the child,
put down the child, or hurt the child.
Help parents to create an atmosphere
of peace, safety, kindness, and affirmation,
so that each child grows up in peace
to become who you created them to be—
your holy peacemakers.

Please inspire spouses to be nonviolent to each other,
that they may model the nonviolent life
for their children
and help hasten your new world of nonviolence.

Every house in the world is filled with violence.
We need your Holy Spirit of nonviolence
to come upon every household
so that families become more peaceful and nonviolent.
We need families of peace, love, and nonviolence.

You have created the human race
around the family unit.

But everything, including the family,
has become infected with violence.
Send your Holy Spirit upon us
that nonviolence might become the norm of every family,
the ultimate family value.

Help parents, children, siblings, and relatives
to choose nonviolence and create nonviolent families,
and then raise up a new generation
who will pursue nonviolence as the new norm
for every culture and society.
I ask this in the name of the nonviolent Jesus.

Amen.

Show the World the Power of Gospel Nonviolence

Dear God,

In the Sermon on the Mount,
Jesus rejected the ancient teaching of
"an eye for an eye, and a tooth for a tooth."
Like Gandhi, he knew that retaliatory violence
would only make the whole world blind and toothless.
Instead, he commanded us to "offer no violent resistance
to one who does evil."
Turn the other cheek,
offer your cloak,
go the extra mile,
and give to those who ask.

For Jesus, nonviolence is creative,
while violence is totally predictable.
He wants us to break the downward spiral of violence,
non-cooperate with violence,
and begin practicing nonviolence
as a new methodology for social change,
a new way of life
so that everyone could live life to the fullest.

Dear God, I believe Jesus was right,
that this teaching is the greatest,
most important lesson for humanity,
that his way is our only hope,
our only way forward.
You call us to love unconditionally,
to show compassion,
and to make peace,
but to do so within the boundaries of nonviolence—
that we will not hurt or kill one another ever again.

But dear God,
very few human beings believe in nonviolence,

much less try to practice it!
Most don't know anything about it.
Few can even conceive of it.
The churches long ago rejected your way of nonviolence.
Few teach this important Gospel lesson.

Please help us.
Inspire us to reconsider
this Gospel commandment of nonviolence;
to rediscover the nonviolence of Jesus;
to experiment with this teaching;
to become people of nonviolence;
and to envision ways to institutionalize nonviolence
in our institutions, nations, and world.

This is possible, but we need political will,
so that nations would fund nonviolent conflict resolution
as the legitimate, legal way to resolve conflict.

Hear our prayer,
that we might experience these breakthroughs.
Show the world the power of Gospel nonviolence,
that billions of people will embrace
your way of nonviolence,
that we might build grassroots movements
of nonviolence to abolish war, weapons,
poverty, racism, and systemic injustice,
and welcome your reign of nonviolence here on earth.

Thank you,
God of nonviolence,
for hearing my prayer.

Amen.

In Your Universal Compassion and Mercy, Everyone Is Redeemable

Dear God,

In your infinite compassion and mercy,
you reach out with love toward every human being.
Help us to show your compassion and mercy widely,
especially toward those we're told are not worthy of
compassion or mercy.

This is one of our greatest needs today—
how to show compassion and mercy to everyone,
especially those we marginalize and discriminate against.
Give us the grace to understand
the wisdom of universal compassion and mercy,
within the framework and boundary of nonviolence,
that we might create more compassionate societies.

No one stands outside the reach
of your compassion and mercy.
In your universal compassion and mercy,
you insist that everyone is redeemable,
everyone deserves another chance,
everyone can accept your wisdom of peace.

In Jesus, you show us the heights
of compassion and mercy.
In Jesus, you model the ideal
of universal compassion and mercy.
You show us how we can live humanly.

Send us his spirit that we might break through
our prejudices and narrow-mindedness,
widen our vision to embrace the whole human race
and make compassion and mercy the human standard.

May we never exclude anyone ever again.

May we include everyone in compassion,
mercy, love, and peace.
May we institutionalize compassion and inclusivity
that war and killings might cease,
and equality and justice become the norm,
that we can create new cultures of peace,
compassion, and nonviolence.

Thank you.
Amen.

Jesus Tells Us to Pray for Our Persecutors, So Here Goes

Dear God,

In the Sermon on the Mount,
Jesus commands us to love our enemies,
and then he tells us to pray for our persecutors.
So here goes.

I pray for everyone who opposes
the work of justice and disarmament,
who maintains systemic injustice and harms creation,
who hinders your reign of nonviolence and peace on earth.
I pray that you will convert them
to the wisdom of nonviolence and universal love,
widen their hearts to embrace the whole human family,
and direct them on the path of peace.

I pray for all warmakers and soldiers,
those who organize the deaths of millions
of your suffering people from Iraq, Afghanistan,
and Palestine to Haiti, Sudan, and Syria,
those who ignore the cry of the poor
from Africa to Latin America, who serve the superrich,
and lead the world to the brink of destruction.
Convert them all to your way of nonviolence.

Bless all the generals, the commanders, the bombers,
the bombmakers, the pilots, the obedient soldiers,
the recruiters, the marines, the torturers,
the CIA agents, the suicidal terrorists,
all those who kill people,
who promote killing,
who organize killing,
who order killing,
who fund killing,
who serve the forces of death.

Bless all those stuck in hate groups,
all the neo-Nazis and KKK members,
that they will come to their senses and leave.
Touch them. Disarm them. Wake them up.
Make them stop their violence and turn them around.
Convert them all to your way of nonviolence.

Bless those law-abiding, obedient citizens
who build and maintain nuclear weapons
at Los Alamos, Livermore Labs,
Oak Ridge, and elsewhere,
that they might quit their jobs and disarm.
Bless those who guard the nuclear bunkers,
manage them, and prepare to push the button,
that they might quit their jobs and disarm.
Bless the executioners on death row,
the judges who sentence people to death,
the lawyers and prosecutors who legalize murder.
Convert them all to your way of nonviolence,
that the big business of death might come to an end.

Bless all the senators, congress people, governors,
Chief Justices and all those in the Executive Branch
who run the American empire.
Bless all Wall Street brokers, bankers, businessmen,
and corporate executives who reap a massive profit
off the poverty, misery, squalor, hunger,
and death of the world's poor.
Bless all the brutalizing prison guards,
all police officers, FBI agents, immigration agents,
marshals, sheriffs, and law officers
who hurt and imprison your victimized people.
Convert them all to your way of nonviolence,
that the greed and misery might end,
that justice and equality might come true.

Bless those who destroy the earth,
who bulldoze the rainforests,

who run the logging companies,
who drill for oil, who pollute the air, poison the oceans,
destroy the artic, hunt your creatures, destroy the ozone,
operate nuclear power plants, radiate your land,
risk global warming, and spread the plague of cancer
through their nuclear industries.
Convert them all to your way of nonviolence,
that we might honor the land and her creatures,
and protect and respect all creation.

Bless all the chaplains who serve the war machine,
all the mean priests, bully ministers,
law and order bishops and cardinals,
who bless war and serve the idols of war,
who punish and condemn,
who refuse to welcome and forgive,
who seek control and domination instead of your reign
of justice, equality, and peace.
Convert them all to your way of nonviolence,
that they might renounce power and control,
side with the poor, and speak out
for justice and disarmament.

Forgive them all.
They know not what they do.

May we all be converted
to the way and wisdom of nonviolence.
Bless us all, that we might become peacemakers,
your beloved sons and daughters
who herald the coming of your reign of peace,
a new world without war, hunger, poverty,
injustice, nuclear weapons,
or environmental destruction,
that we might all dwell in your peace.

Amen.

Hasten the Day When There Are No More Victims or Victimizers

Dear God,

I pray for all those in prison,
the millions of brothers and sisters around the world
who languish behind bars,
many of them suffering unjustly,
many of them lost forever to their families,
many of them tortured and crushed,
many of them without legal assistance,
many of them stuck without any recourse
to justice or mercy.

I pray for a miracle that the world's prisons
will be reformed,
that every guard and prisoner will be taught
nonviolence and civility,
that nonviolent offenders will be released,
and that justice systems will be set up with fairness.
Most of all, I pray that prisoners everywhere will get
the therapy, treatment,
and healing rehabilitation they need
to reclaim their humanity in freedom.

In the meantime, inspire more and more people
to reach out to prisoners to heal them
of loneliness, violence, and despair.
Bring educators into prisons to teach
prisoners the way of nonviolence.
Grant doctors and nurses access
to heal the physical needs of every person
in prison around the world.
Make prisons more just, more nonviolent, more human,
so that prisoners will be healed and disarmed
for release to serve humanity.

Most of all, help us educate every child in the world
in your way of nonviolent conflict resolution
so that one day violent crime becomes rare
and prisons, too, are abolished.

May every victim of violence be healed
and learn to forgive their perpetrators,
and may every perpetrator be healed and do atonement,
so that together we hasten the day
when there are no more victims or victimizers,
only nonviolent brothers and sisters everywhere.

Amen.

For All the Sick and Dying People Around the World

Dear God,

I pray for all the sick and dying people around the world,
that they may be healed, comforted,
and given the grace of your healing peace.
Please take care of them, be with them,
touch them, heal them, and comfort them.
Take away their fear,
help them to be at peace with their situation,
and send them loving friends and relatives
to care for them and be with them
in their time of suffering, at the hour of their death.

So many sisters and brothers around the world
are suffering and dying!
I pray for every one of them—
for my own relatives and friends,
all the people I have met on my journey,
all the people I admire and have taught me
by their example—
all those who are suffering and dying.

I pray for all those who die in accidents,
car crashes, plane crashes, and natural disasters,
all those who die in floods, tornadoes, earthquakes,
hurricanes, fires, tsunamis, and mudslides,
all those who suffer and die.

But I also pray for the nameless masses,
the countless millions of unknown
suffering and dying people who have no money,
no food, no medicine, and no friends,
who have lived and died in abject poverty.
I pray, dear God, for the child starving to death
in a refugee camp in Africa,
or some tiny village in India or Latin America.

I pray for the mother dying in poverty,
the father dying in prison,
the ones dying alone in pain and despair.
Be with them, heal them, and if they die,
welcome them immediately into paradise.
May they rejoice, may they rise in peace!

I imagine the poorest person on the planet,
the one suffering and dying all alone,
all but forgotten, like Jesus on the cross.
Send your Holy Spirit upon that person
and let him or her know that you love them,
that they are not alone,
that they can be at peace
and feel your consoling presence
and know that they are headed toward an eternity
of peace and joy in your loving presence.

Inspire us to create a more just and peaceful world,
so that no one suffers and dies an unjust, lonely death,
that we might make it possible
for everyone to live and die in peace.

Today, like every other day,
some 200,000 people will die.
That should be the headline of every newspaper
around the world every day.
But we pretend no one is dying, no one ever dies,
that death doesn't exist or matter.

I pray for every one of them.
Bless them, touch them, give them peace,
and welcome them with open arms
into your eternal home of peace and joy.
And someday, when my hour comes,
welcome me home, too.

Amen.

Help Us Reject Death as a Social Methodology

Dear God,

I beg you for the miracle
of the abolition of the death penalty.
Please help us to stop executing prisoners,
and to start helping those who are permanently damaged
by death row through healing rehabilitation.

No good comes from executing people.
It does not bring healing or justice;
it only brings further death.
The death penalty system is unjust, racist, and unfair.
Killing people who kill people is not the way
to teach people not to kill people.

Most of all, it violates your law of loving nonviolence.

The nonviolent Jesus prevented the execution
of a woman caught in adultery
and issued a new commandment:
"Let the one without sin
be the first to throw a stone at her."
He refused to condemn her,
he sided with the condemned,
and then he became one with the condemned.
Jesus was put on death row
and executed as an unredeemable criminal.

When we execute those on death row,
we execute Christ all over again.

Inspire us to forgive those who have hurt us,
or even killed our loved ones.
Help us to stop executing people,
and to stop murdering one another.

Give us the grace to become people of nonviolence,
so that gun violence and killings stop,
that we might help heal each other
and reclaim our inner peace.
Give us a world without vengeance, retaliation,
retribution, or state-sanctioned murder,
a new world of nonviolence
where we can prepare each other
for the nonviolent coming
of your kingdom of nonviolence.

God of peace, help us reject death
as a social methodology.

Help us to live life to the fullest
and let others live life to the fullest,
so that no one is ever killed again,
and nonviolence becomes the law of the land.

Amen.

Inspire the World to Reach Out and Help
the World's Refugees

Dear God,

I beg you to help the over 60 million refugees
and displaced peoples around the world,
the highest number since World War II.
They do not want to leave their homes, their livelihoods,
their relatives, or their nations,
but they are forced to, against their will,
because of violence, terror, and war.
In fleeing the violence,
they choose not to join the violence,
but their lives are uprooted and traumatized.
I beg you to inspire the world
to reach out and help refugees,
and to end the violence from which they flee.

Over 22 million people have been displaced
or killed in Syria in recent years.
It's hard to take in such numbers,
so I pray for sisters and brothers such as Dora,
a young Syrian woman, who along with her fiancé,
recently fled the horrific killings and war
in her hometown in Syria.
They joined six million others
making the journey to Cairo, Egypt,
where they struggled for a year in despair and poverty.
One day, Dora's fiancé said they had to take the chance
and get to Europe if they were going to survive.
So they used their life savings to buy tickets on a ship
to smuggle them across the Mediterranean Sea to Italy.

Hundreds of people—
women, children, older people,
all in the same dire predicament—
were crowded onto the boat.
For four terrible days, they suffered in the rough seas
with no food and little water. Then suddenly, armed men

approached in a small boat, threatened them,
and attacked their ship, which capsized.
Hundreds drowned. Others floated in the sea for days.
One by one, many died.

Dora's fiancé said to her in tears,
"I love you so much, you are the love of my life,
but I don't have any more strength,"
and he slipped into the water
and drowned in front of her.
Another woman holding up a tiny baby
thrust the baby into Dora's hands and said,
"I can't swim any more. Take my baby
and get her to safety."
Then she too slipped into the water and died.

After 48 hours, Dora and a few others were rescued.
Eventually she and the baby were brought to a place
in northern Europe where they are being cared for.

Every refugee needs our loving hospitality, our loving care,
and our healing help so they can start their lives over.
This hospitality and care is supposed to be
the hallmark of the peacemaking Church,
of the Christian life.

Dear God, inspire and mobilize Christians
and people of good will everywhere, including me,
to do what we can to reach out with loving hospitality
and care to our sisters and brothers in need,
to work to end this global crisis of refugees,
and to stop the causes of this catastrophe
by working for an end to war, violence,
poverty, systemic injustice, and environmental destruction.

Thank you, on behalf of Dora and all refugees,
for hearing this prayer.

Amen.

Part Four:

For All Creatures

How varied are your works, O God;
in wisdom you have wrought them all.
The earth is full of your creatures.
Look at the sea, great and wide.
It teems with countless beings,
Living things both large and small.
All these look to you.

–Psalm 104:24-27

Through Your Creatures, You Teach Us How to Be Human

Dear God,

Thank you for all the amazing and varied creatures
that you have created,
who live today across the planet.

In your infinite creativity and generosity,
you have made every imaginable form of life.
In the oceans, you have created everything
from the tiniest fish to the majestic whale,
sea turtles and dolphins,
hammerhead sharks and manta rays,
lobsters and crabs,
octopuses and otters.

In the air, you put a million glorious birds,
from robins and sparrows
to hummingbirds and toucans,
from black crows to white doves,
hawks to vultures,
eagles to Steller's jays.
You created millions of insects and every type of tiny
crawling creature.

You give us marvelous, majestic wild animals—
lions, giraffes, rhinoceroses,
elk, deer, tigers,
bears, bobcats, and coyotes.

And you give us the creatures we have
welcomed into our lives,
such as horses, dogs, cats,
hamsters, and goldfish.
Through these creatures, you show us

your loving generosity,
and through them, you teach us how to be human.

Thank you for your generosity and kindness
by giving us these amazing companions on earth,
and for showing us how to live
in your peaceable kingdom
by watching them.

Inspire us to listen and learn from your creatures,
that we might find you in them,
and learn to live in peace together.

Amen.

Help Us Protect Your Holy Creatures, Not Kill Them

Dear God,

You placed us in this magnificent Garden of Eden,
and you gave us dominion over your creatures
and your creation.
Thank you for this undeserved gift, this Garden of Eden,
all the beautiful creatures, and this holy,
once-in-a-lifetime opportunity
to share it all together in peace.

But dear God, we have killed your creatures by the billions
and we go on destroying Mother Earth.
Wake us up before it is too late,
that the killings may stop,
that all creatures and all creation will be protected,
that we might all live together in your peace.

Help us to protect your holy creatures,
that we may learn to be nonviolent to them,
that we might not kill them,
that we might not bring them to extinction.

We know now, dear God, that for the first time,
millions upon millions of creatures have become extinct,
just within the last one hundred years,
because of our corporate greed
and the way we pollute and destroy the earth.
Awaken us to understand what we have done,
to grieve the extinctions we have caused,
and to change ourselves
so that no more creatures are killed or become extinct.

Help me do my part, dear God,
that I might be nonviolent to all creatures,
that I might be more mindful about how I participate
in the extinction of your creatures

and non-cooperate with that violence,
that I might join the movements
to protect your creatures and creation.

In my own life, guide me to a new awareness
about the food I eat,
the clothing I wear,
and the products I purchase,
so that I do not harm your creatures ever again.
Motivate me to learn about and support
policies and laws that protect
your creatures and your creation.

Most of all, dear God,
protect your creatures and Mother Earth from us.
Don't let us destroy them.
Make us stop our ecological violence
and change us to live in right nonviolent relationship
with all your creatures and your beautiful creation.

Amen.

Part Five:

For Creation

Let the heavens be glad and the earth rejoice;
Let the sea and what fills it resound;
Let the plains be joyful and all that is in them.
Then let all the trees of the forest rejoice
Before the Lord who comes to govern the earth,
To govern the world with justice
and the people with faithfulness.

–Psalm 96:11-13

Help Us Stop the Destruction of the Earth

Dear God,

I pray for Mother Earth.
Please intervene and stop our ongoing destruction
of the environment, land, water, and air.
It's as if we are drunkards, oblivious of our actions,
destroying our own home.
The nations of the world seem determined
to extract fossil fuels and any resource
that will bring more money,
regardless of the consequences of our actions
upon the earth, the poor, or future generations.

At this rate, we will unleash unlimited carbon,
raise the earth's temperature, melt the polar ice caps,
and unleash catastrophic climate change
with unparalleled hurricanes, tornadoes,
floods, fires, and droughts,
as well as the deaths of millions,
the loss of clean drinking water,
and a global hell of permanent war,
starvation, and refugees.

Dear God, prevent us from causing
this ongoing crucifixion of the earth.
Help us to stop the destruction of the earth.
Help us to be nonviolent to the earth.

Give us the wisdom to share the earth wisely,
to protect our water, land, and air,
to leave fossil fuels in the ground
and pursue alternative forms of energy,
such as wind and solar power.

Give us a new understanding that we might put
Mother Earth and her creatures first,

that we might also protect the poor and vulnerable,
that we might legislate global protection
of the environment
and stop greedy corporations
from raping Mother Earth
and killing her poor.

Dear God,
you gave us this Garden of Eden as your gift,
with the commandment to treat her
nonviolently and respectfully
so that everyone might live in peace
"underneath their own vine and fig tree."

We have completely broken your covenant,
set out to destroy your Garden,
and lost our souls along the way.
We repent of our environmental destruction.
Wake humanity up now
that we might all treat one another
and creation nonviolently,
that we might restore creation and honor your gift.
Hear our prayer.

Amen.

Build A New Global Grassroots Movement
to Stop the Destruction of Mother Earth

Dear God,

If the nations of the world continue
on their destructive path toward environmental destruction
and catastrophic climate change,
then your creation is surely doomed.
But through the nonviolent Jesus,
you gave us a power to resist evil
through active nonviolence.
Our hope lies then in your organized grassroots
movements of active nonviolence.
Raise up sisters and brothers by the billions
who work day and night to protect creation.
Build a new global grassroots movement
to stop the destruction of Mother Earth
and her creatures.

Creator God, anything is possible with you.
We are sorry for our environmental destruction.
We grieve the damage and death we have caused.
We repent of our environmental violence,
our hatred of the poor,
of your creatures,
of your creation.
Our violence is our own self destruction.
We have gone insane.
Give us the sanity of nonviolence.

Give us a new will,
a new spirit,
a new heart,
a new grassroots movement to protect creation,
that we might respect and protect creation
and create a new culture of nonviolence for Mother Earth.

We love you for the gift of your creation,
for the beauty of Mother Earth.
Thank you for such a gift.
Do not let us destroy it.
Do not let the nations of the world burn it down,
wage permanent war,
and kill millions of sisters and brothers
along the way.

Give us the wisdom and way forward,
that we might become who you created us to be—
your loving stewards of your beautiful paradise.

Amen.

Part Six:

For the Global Grassroots Movements for Peace and Justice

In days to come, the mountain of God's house
shall be established as the highest mountain
and raised above the hills.
All nations shall stream toward it.
Many people shall come and say,
"Come, let us climb God's mountain,
to the house of the God of Jacob,
that God may instruct us in God's ways,
that we may walk in God's paths."
For from Zion shall go forth instruction,
and the word of God from Jerusalem.
God shall judge between the nations,
and impose terms on many peoples.
They shall beat their swords into plowshares
and their spears into pruning hooks.
One nation shall not raise the sword against another,
nor shall they train for war ever again.

–Isaiah 2:2-4

Bless All the Grassroots Movements of Nonviolence Around the World

Dear God,

Please bless all the thousands
of grassroots movements
of nonviolence around the world
that struggle for justice, disarmament, and peace
for humanity and creation.

Jesus himself was a movement organizer,
and led his disciples on a nonviolent campaign
from Galilee to Jerusalem,
sending messengers ahead of him
to prepare for his coming
and to announce his reign of peace.
In Jerusalem, he confronted the empire
with nonviolent direction action,
and was arrested and killed for that,
but his nonviolent movement lived on.

Jesus' grassroots campaign of nonviolence
continued down through the ages,
from the desert fathers and mothers,
to the Benedictine monasteries
and the Franciscan communities,
to the Quakers and Mennonites,
and then the Abolitionists, the Suffragists,
India's Independence movement led by Gandhi,
and the Civil Rights movement led by Dr. King.

Today, there are thousands of grassroots movements
around the world where ordinary people carry on
Jesus' campaign of nonviolence.
Please hear their prayers, protect them,
give them courage and strength,
and if it be your will,

give them the victory of justice
and nonviolent transformation.

Let us see the power and wisdom of Gospel nonviolence
at work in the world today in
your grassroots movements
of nonviolence made up of ordinary people.
Give us new breakthroughs of justice,
disarmament and protection of creation.

Send us forth anew,
as the nonviolent Jesus sent his 72 disciples,
"like lambs into the midst of wolves"
to proclaim the coming of your reign,
a whole new world of nonviolence, justice, and peace.

Through your grassroots movements,
disarm your world,
give us your justice,
protect Mother Earth and her creatures,
and help us all join Jesus' campaign of nonviolence
until you reign on earth as you reign in heaven.

Amen.

Help Me to Serve the Global Grassroots
Movement of Nonviolence

Dear God,

Help me to serve your reign of peace
by serving the global grassroots movement of nonviolence
for the coming of your reign of peace here on earth.

Make me an instrument of your peace,
that I might do my small part to help abolish
war, poverty, hunger, executions, nuclear weapons,
systemic injustice, and environmental destruction,
to make your nonviolent reign of peace
more palpable everywhere.

But more, help me when I'm discouraged,
when I think there's no hope,
when I give up on others and give up on myself,
when I sense the dread of despair and apathy
sneaking up on me. Raise me up, keep me going, use me
for your work for justice and peace,
and most of all, keep me faithful
to the lifelong journey of justice and peace.

Let my entire life be a struggle for justice and peace,
one long campaign for a new world of nonviolence.
Let my life bear tremendous good fruit for others,
and inspire others to join that struggle.
Give me good cheer, a good heart,
a sense of humor, a spirit of peace and love,
and that revolutionary patience needed
for the lifelong, long-haul work of peacemaking.

Help me like the saints and prophets of old
to live a full life in your service of justice and peace
that I may join them one day in that place
where the nonviolent revolution has come true
and is permanent, that together,
we might all praise you and your boundless peace.

Amen.

Build Up a Global Grassroots Movement
for the Abolition of War and Nuclear Weapons

Dear God of Peace,

I ask you for the greatest miracle,
the biggest prayer, the most impossible gift:
the abolition of war, weapons, and nuclear weapons.
You are not a god of war, you are the God of peace.
You are not a god of violence or vengeance,
but the living God of nonviolence and reconciliation.
You are not a god of hate, but the God of universal love.

You hate our wars, and grieve the madness
of militarism and killing.
You anguish over the hundreds of millions
of men, women, and children
who have been slaughtered down
through the ages in our collective insanity.
You weep over the annihilation
of hundreds of thousands of people
in Hiroshima and Nagasaki,
and curse the tens of thousands of nuclear weapons
we have built since then.
You turn away from our liturgies, prayers,
and blessings of war and our weapons.
You side with our victims, with the children,
with all those who are shot, bombed, and obliterated.

Give us a spirit of steadfast opposition to war,
that we might dedicate our lives and build
a new global grassroots movement
for the abolition of war.
Inspire the people of the world
to refuse the wars of the nations,
to non-cooperate with them,
to put down their guns,
to end the wars.

Help us not to make war,
not to vote for war,
not to pay for war,
not to send our children off to war,
not to bless our wars,
and not to justify our wars.

In particular, lead your churches and religions
to reject every aspect of war,
weapons, and nuclear weapons.
Make your churches and religions voices
for disarmament and the abolition of war.
Inspire every priest, minister, bishop,
cardinal, rabbi, nun, and imam
to oppose war, violence, and nuclear weapons,
and to espouse nonviolence and peace.

Raise up a new generation of prophets of peace
who will lead us to abolish war
and the causes of war once and for all.

God of peace, give us the sanity of peace and nonviolence
that we might not destroy one another and your creation.
Help us to reject the idolatry of weapons,
that we might worship you as the living God of peace
and be your faithful servants and apostles of peace.

Amen.

Help Us to Eradicate Hunger, Extreme Poverty, and Unjust Suffering

Dear God,

Billions of sisters and brothers suffer today
in extreme poverty,
with inadequate housing, food, clean water,
employment, education, healthcare, or dignity.
The numbers will increase exponentially
as wars and catastrophic climate change
deepen and worsen.

You pledged that whatever we do to the poor and
oppressed, we do to you.
You announced that you are fully present
in the hungry, thirsty, naked,
homeless, sick, and imprisoned,
and that you want us to serve you
in their poverty and oppression,
and to work for the abolition of poverty, hunger,
and unjust suffering.

We do what we can in our own limited way.
Help us to reach out to the poor and disenfranchised,
to serve you among them and relieve their suffering.

But more, give us a global miracle.
Help us to eradicate hunger, extreme poverty,
and unjust suffering.
Awaken in humanity a new global conscience
to end the suffering and oppression
of our sisters and brothers across the planet.

Disarm the nations so they spend trillions of dollars
not on weapons of war, but on food,
housing and healthcare for the world's poor,

that everyone may share in the basics of human life
and live in peace with social, economic,
and racial justice.
Inspire the handful of billionaires who have more money
than half of the human race to give their money
and resources to the world's poor
for the elimination of extreme poverty.

We pray, beloved God,
for our beloved sisters and brothers
around the world who suffer in total powerlessness
without food, healthcare, housing, clean water,
or the basics of life.
We pray for them that their needs may be met,
that they may know justice and the fullness of life,
that you may be glorified
through the abolition of poverty.
Thank you for hearing our prayer.

Amen.

A Prayer for an End to Gun Violence

Dear God,

Please send your healing Holy Spirit among us
that we will end the horrific epidemic of gun violence,
that the killings might stop,
and that we all might become more nonviolent.

In recent years,
we have suffered
mass killings,
street killings,
accidental killings,
and suicides from guns.

We grieve for all those killed and injured
through gun violence,
especially in massacres such as
the Las Vegas concert shooting
where 58 were killed and over 500 injured;
the Pulse nightclub shooting in Orlando
where 49 were killed and 53 injured;
the San Bernardino, CA office shooting
where 14 were killed and 17 injured;
the Oregon community college shooting
where ten were killed;
the Charleston, SC church shooting,
where nine were killed;
the Aurora, CO movie theater shooting
where 12 were killed and 70 injured;
the Sandy Hook elementary school shooting
where 26 were killed;
the Virginia Tech shooting
where 32 were killed;
and the San Antonio, TX church massacre,
where 26 were killed, and another 20 wounded.

Long ago, Jesus said that
"Those who live by the sword will die by the sword."
We have become people who live by the gun,
and so we are people who are dying by the gun.
Our culture of violence is so sick
that senseless gun killings have become normal.

We beg for a spiritual conversion of heart
from gun violence to Gospel nonviolence.
We beg for a healing conversion
from the sick dependence on guns
and temptation to do violence with guns
to the transformation of disarmament
and healing nonviolence.
We beg for a political conversion from
the National Rifle Association political power
and the unbridled corporate greed
of the gun manufacturers
to the end of all gun violence as our political priority.
We beg for a cultural conversion from a culture of guns
to a culture of nonviolence and gunlessness.

Inspire us to do what we can to end these killings—
to end the political control
of the National Rifle Association;
to stop the corporate greed behind
the gun manufacturers and the NRA
which leads to rampant gun violence and countless deaths;
to set new laws requiring background checks
and safety procedures; and
to end the proliferation and use of handguns.

We ask for the grace that gun manufacturers and NRA
members renounce the greed behind the pro-gun
movement and pursue practical gun control legislation;
that we might all put down our guns and disarm;
that we might find our security in nonviolent love
for one another and in God;

and that we might all find
our identity not in gun ownership
but in living nonviolently
as your beloved sons and daughters.

May we all renounce violence and take new steps
toward a culture of nonviolence
where no one gets killed,
where no one has a gun,
where everyone practices nonviolence
toward everyone else.

Amen.

Part Seven:

For the World

Thus says God the Lord,
who created the heavens and stretched them out,
who spread out the earth with its crops,
who gives breath to its people
and spirit to those who walk on it:
I, the Lord, have called you for the victory of justice,
I have grasped you by the hand;
I formed you, and set you as a covenant of the people,
a light for the nations,
to open the eyes of the blind,
to bring out prisoners from confinement,
and from the dungeon, those who live in darkness.

–Isaiah 42:5-7

For All Sisters and Brothers on the Continent of Africa

Dear God,

I pray for all sisters and brothers on the continent of Africa,
where so many suffer poverty and deprivation,
but where so many live life to the depths
in the ancient wisdom of love.
From the deserts to the mountains,
from the rivers to the savannahs,
Africa beats to the rhythm of life.
Bless Mother Africa.

With 54 nations, 1.2 billion people,
and over a thousand languages,
it is the youngest continent, with a median age of 19.
It is filled with life—
the wild animals,
the glorious vistas,
the music and culture,
the sharing of food and community,
the mixture of tribes, ethnicities, and cultures.

And yet, it has been dominated for centuries
by the nations of the north,
who kidnapped and killed
millions of sisters and brothers for slavery.
Even today, in times of independence and
decolonialization, the violence continues.
Racism, corruption, greed, AIDS, disease, war, hunger,
illiteracy, deforestation, and even genocide continue.
Over five million brothers and sisters
have died so far in the horrific war in Congo.

Give us an end to the oppression
and domination of Africa.
End its wars, famines, poverty, and genocide.

Let a new dawn bring a new day for Africa,
that it might be the continent of nonviolence,
where everyone can share in the fullness of life,
justice, and peace with dignity and all their needs met.
May the healing, unifying spirit of ubuntu,
I am because you are,
spread around the world.

Thank you.
Amen.

For All Sisters and Brothers in Latin America

Dear God,

I pray for all sisters and brothers in Latin America,
for all those stuck in dire poverty
from Mexico and Haiti to Peru and Chile.
Thank you for the beauty of these people,
for this land, for their free spirit.
Touch them and heal them
that they may embrace Jesus' way
of nonviolence and justice,
that they may renounce greed,
death squads, and dictatorships,
that they may create a new culture of peace.

Thank you for the beautiful saints and martyrs
who have marked this landscape.
Thank you for all those who have stood up
against systemic injustice,
thank you for those who have given their lives
for justice and creation,
thank you for the many grassroots movements
that have sown the seeds of hope and peace
throughout Latin America.

God of peace, bless Latin America—
its nineteen nations,
626 million people, especially its indigenous.
Such a long history—
of poverty and imperial domination,
Spanish and Portuguese conquest,
colonialism and slavery,
US-backed dictatorships and death squads,
to independence and new breakthroughs for justice.

Haiti remains one of the poorest places in the world,
on the doorstep of the richest nation on earth.
In Mexico, the daily killings by drug lords,
their death squads, and gang members terrorize millions.
The gang killings are increasing in El Salvador,
the rainforests of the Amazon are being destroyed,
corporate greed still reigns,
and hundreds of millions suffer and die.
Heal them all.
Grant peace, disarmament, and a new spirit
of nonviolence to one and all!

You love the people and land of Latin America!
Bless them abundantly.
Guide them to turn a new corner toward
justice, disarmament, and peace.
Give them new cultures of nonviolence
that honors everyone and Mother Earth herself.

Take care of your children and your creation
in Latin America.
Teach them to put down the gun.
Make them a sign of hope and peace
for the rest of the world,
that we might all learn
from their long nonviolent struggle,
and join your campaign for a new world of peace.

I ask this through the intercession
of Blessed Oscar Romero
and Our Lady of Guadalupe.

Amen.

For All Sisters and Brothers Throughout Asia

Dear God,

Please bless all sisters and brothers throughout Asia,
from the war-torn lands of Gaza, Syria, and Iraq,
through India, Pakistan, and Afghanistan,
to Russia, China, and Japan.
These are your people, dear God.
Give them a new spirit of peace,
nonviolence and justice,
that they may turn toward you and one another
and pursue a new culture of justice and nonviolence.

Asia includes 30% of the earth's land
and 4.4 billion sisters and brothers.
Their cultures vary from Israel and Saudi Arabia
to Pakistan and China
to Japan and the Philippines.
Your people are so different,
but they are all your beautiful children,
each with their own problems, social sins, and injustices,
each with their own hopes, blessings, and possibilities.

I ask your blessings upon the people of China,
for an end to their pollution and suffering;
upon the people of India,
for an end to their poverty and suffering;
upon the people of Russia,
for an end to their oppression, injustice, and suffering;
for all the peoples of Pakistan, Afghanistan, Iraq, Syria,
Palestine, and Yemen,
for an end to the wars, bombings, US drone attacks,
oppressions, ISIS and Al Qaeda terrorism and killings,
that they might renounce violence,
turn toward nonviolence,
and start to build new cultures
of nonviolence and peace.

I pray for everyone in Asia—
for those who suffer poverty
and death squad killings in the Philippines;
those who suffer poverty and repression in North Korea;
to those who suffer endless war
in Syria, Iraq, and Afghanistan;
that you will build up their grassroots
movements of nonviolence;
that you will instill a new spirit of hope and peace;
and that one morning, a new day of peace with justice
will dawn over Asia.

God of peace, God of Asia,
touch your suffering people,
heal them and give them new peace.
May their long dark night
of suffering and oppression end,
and a new day of liberation, justice, and peace begin.
This is your will.
May it come true.

And dear God, bless all your islanders,
including the people of Australia and New Zealand;
and bless and protect the Arctic Circle and Antarctica,
that the ice sheets might not melt,
that the creatures will survive,
that Mother Earth will heal.

Thank you for hearing this prayer.

Amen.

Part Eight:

For Mature Discipleship to the Nonviolent Jesus

Blessed are the peacemakers . . . .
Offer no violent resistance to one who does evil . . . .
Love your enemies and pray for your persecutors . . . .
Seek first God's reign and God's justice,
and everything will be provided for you . . . .
Enter through the narrow gate.

–Matthew 5-7, the Sermon on the Mount

If anyone wishes to come after me,
they must deny themselves,
and take up their cross daily and follow me.

–Luke 9:23

Help Me to Become a Mature, Authentic Disciple
of the Nonviolent Jesus

Dear God,

We Christians have strayed so far
from the nonviolent Jesus
and his teachings of nonviolence.
We have justified war, waged war,
held human beings as slaves,
burned women at the stake,
built and dropped nuclear weapons,
tortured and executed people,
nurtured violence, and in general,
done everything possible to maintain
the culture of violence and war.

And yet, Jesus was totally nonviolent!
He practiced nonviolence, taught nonviolence,
and envisioned a new world of nonviolence
which he called, "the Kingdom of God at hand."
We go to church to fulfill our Sunday obligations,
but live our daily lives
as if Jesus' spectacular nonviolence
has no influence on our lives.

Dear God, I want to start all over again.
I want to hear the nonviolent Jesus call me
to follow him as his disciple on the path
of peace, love, and nonviolence.
Help me to read his Gospels,
to spend time in prayer with him,
and to act on his teachings
that my life might more and more resemble
his gentle, loving, nonviolent life.

Help me to become a mature, authentic disciple
of the nonviolent Jesus.

More, let me too become one of his apostles
of peace, love, and nonviolence to the world.
Take away my hypocrisy.
Lead me on the path of humility,
kindness, and gentleness,
that I might share your love and wisdom with others,
inspire others to follow the nonviolent Jesus,
and prepare a new way for him by working
for a new culture of peace and nonviolence
here on earth.

And then, dear God,
help all of us to grow up,
and become mature disciples of the nonviolent Jesus,
your holy people of Gospel nonviolence.

Thank you.
Amen.

Give Me the Grace to Live My Life
According to Your Beatitudes

Dear God,

Help me to live according to Jesus' Beatitudes,
the core beginning teachings of his
Sermon on the Mount (Matthew 5:1-12).
Give me the grace to let go of money,
possessions, pride, and privilege,
to become vulnerable and open to you,
to accept my poverty of spirit and dependence on you,
and set off on your way of peace, love,
justice, and nonviolence.
That way, I will always need you
and live in your reign of peace and love,
from now on.

Bless me as I grow in compassion for others,
that I might feel new empathy and love for everyone,
especially the poor, oppressed, and mournful.
As millions suffer and die each year
from war, poverty, and unjust disease,
let me mourn for them.
Let me mourn for all the creatures we destroy,
and for the ways we destroy the environment.
Then I will feel your consolation.

Bless me that I might not be violent, arrogant, proud,
or part of the domination system.
Instead, help me to be meek, gentle,
nonviolent, and humble,
like your saints, that I may become one with creation
and inherit the earth as my true home,
the promised land of peace.

Bless me that I hunger and thirst for justice
every day of my life,

that I might resist the global systemic injustice
which forces billions of sisters and brothers
into extreme poverty, hunger, illness,
imprisonment, and war.
Give me the satisfaction of a life
spent carrying on your struggle
for justice for the world's poor and oppressed.

Bless me that I might show mercy,
especially toward those the culture deems
unworthy of mercy.
Help me never to withhold mercy,
but to grant clemency to everyone,
to let everyone off the hook,
and to show compassion and respect toward everyone.
That way, I know you will show mercy to me.

Bless me with purity of heart,
with the gift of inner peace and holiness
so everything that comes from within me
might be peaceful, loving, and holy.
Purify my heart, disarm my heart,
fill my heart with your spirit.
Then, I will see you everywhere,
especially in every human being.

Bless me to be your peacemaker.
Help me to renounce violence and war,
to non-cooperate with the culture of war,
to resist war, and serve your global
grassroots movements of nonviolence
to abolish war, injustice, and destruction.
Then I will truly be your beloved child.

Bless me when I am rejected and persecuted
for working for justice and peace,
that I might not retaliate but respond
with love and compassion,

and so always live in your kingdom,
rejoicing like the prophets
of justice and peace through the ages.

Thank you for the Beatitudes.
Give me the grace to live my life
according to your Beatitudes.
Help me to be a Beatitude person,
and teach their blessings far and wide,
so that more and more people
will choose to live according to your Beatitude wisdom.
Help all of us to become Beatitude people.

Amen.

Give Me the Grace to Live Matthew 25,
to Serve You in the Poor, Hungry, Sick, and Dying

Dear God,

According to Matthew 25,
Jesus taught that we will enter your kingdom
on these conditions:
whether or not we fed the hungry,
gave drink to the thirsty,
sheltered the homeless,
welcomed the stranger,
and visited the sick and imprisoned.
He does not say our entrance into eternity
depends on any specific political position,
or our righteousness,
or our sexual purity,
or the fulfillment of any religious obligations.

Jesus announces that how we treated him
in the "distressing disguise" of the poor,
hungry, homeless, sick, and imprisoned
will determine our entrance into heaven.

Give me the grace to spend my days feeding the hungry,
giving drink to the thirsty,
sheltering the homeless,
welcoming the stranger,
and comforting the sick and imprisoned.
More, give me the grace to work for the abolition
of poverty, hunger, homelessness,
unjust disease, and imprisonment.
Help me to end war and all weapons of mass destruction
which not only impoverish millions
and make them hungry, thirsty, sick, and imprisoned,
but which kill people by the millions.

Give me the grace to spend my life
working for a new world
of justice and nonviolence
where every child, every human being,
has food, housing, healthcare, education,
employment, dignity, and respect,
where everyone is trained in nonviolence
so that everyone treats everyone else nonviolently.

Give every Christian this grace,
that we might all become Matthew 25 people.

Dear God,
may Jesus' words come true for me,
my family and friends,
and for everyone.

When that moment comes, be pleased to say,
"Well done, my good and faithful servant.
Come inherit the kingdom of peace, love, and joy
that was prepared for you
from the foundation of the world."

Thank you.
Amen.

For Strength to Follow the Nonviolent Jesus on the Way of the Cross, the Way of Resistance

Dear God,

I wish there was another way forward
than the cross of Jesus,
but that is your will.
Your wisdom is right,
the cross is the way forward,
and so I ask for the grace to carry the cross
in discipleship to the nonviolent Jesus,
that I too might resist systemic injustice and war
and herald the coming of your reign
of peace and nonviolence.

For me, the cross of Jesus is not a flat tire,
a traffic jam, a long line at airport security,
a mean in-law, or some other minor complaint.
The cross of the nonviolent Jesus
is active, daily, nonviolent resistance
to the culture of violence, war, and injustice.
Jesus turned from Galilee
and started his march toward Jerusalem
where he entered the Temple
and turned over the tables of injustice
in an act of nonviolent civil disobedience,
Jesus accepted the consequences
for his revolutionary nonviolence.
That journey, that campaign, that resistance,
has to become the central journey
of our discipleship lives.

Help us resist the structures of violence
as we practice Jesus' steadfast, active nonviolence.
That is the way of the cross.
That is the way forward.

That is our hope, if we are to disarm our world,
create a new culture of peace, and protect creation.

We need to resist the insanity of violence and war,
but we have to use the means of nonviolence
if we want to bring about a nonviolent world.
Every step of that journey will be painful.
We would rather watch TV,
turn away from the struggle, ignore the injustice,
and remain silent in the face
of massive human suffering and death,
but Jesus calls us otherwise.
He wants us to carry on his campaign
of active nonviolence and steadfast resistance
until we wear down the structures of injustice,
convert millions of people to peace,
and welcome a new world of justice,
disarmament, and peace.

This is possible.
This is the power we have been given.
This is the calling he left us.

Dear God, give me the grace to do my part,
to take up my cross daily,
to resist injustice and war
and work for justice and disarmament,
to practice nonviolence and herald a new culture of
nonviolence as Jesus did.

Take away my fear and despair,
give me strength and encouragement,
lead me in the footsteps of Jesus,
and make my life bear the good fruit
of justice, disarmament, and peace for your people.

Amen.

Help Me to Welcome the Risen Jesus' Resurrection Gift of Peace

Dear God,

When Jesus rose from the dead,
he greeted his friends with words of peace,
showed them his wounds,
breathed the Holy Spirit of peace upon them,
and sent them out to continue
his mission of peace and nonviolence.

There was not a trace of revenge, retaliation,
anger, resentment, or bitterness in him.
He was the embodiment of peace.
He was as nonviolent as he always was,
even though we rejected, tortured, and killed him.

Help me to live my life in Jesus' spirit of resurrection.
Let me renounce every trace
of vengeance, retaliation, anger,
resentment, or bitterness;
indeed, wipe away any inclination
toward hatred, violence, or death itself.

Instead, may I always breathe in
his Holy Spirit of peace,
and breathe out his Holy Spirit of peace,
that I may live and walk in his Holy Spirit,
and rejoice in his resurrection.
Help me to welcome his resurrection gift of peace
with all my heart,
and to treasure it every day of my life.

Give me the grace to know that from now on
my survival is already guaranteed,
that as his follower,
I am headed toward the new life of resurrection

in his risen peace.
Let me know in my heart that death
does not get the last word,
that life is stronger than death,
that peace is stronger than war,
that nonviolence is more powerful than violence.

Help me to practice now the resurrection life to come,
that I may not cooperate with the forces of death,
but live in the fullness of life
and help to bring life to others.
Give me faith and courage to go forth into the world
of total violence, war, weapons, and destruction,
with the hope and confidence
that his risen spirit will mobilize us
in grassroots movements of peace and nonviolence
to transform any injustice, end war, torture, and
executions, and abolish nuclear weapons.

Help me to spread Jesus' resurrection
spirit of peace and nonviolence,
that everyone might one day
renounce the forces of death
and welcome Jesus' gift of resurrection peace.

Thank you.
Amen.

Part Nine:

For the Church

Let love be sincere; hate what is evil,
Hold on to what is good.
Love one another with mutual affection;
Anticipate one another in showing honor.
Do not grow slack in zeal, be fervent in spirit,
serve the God of peace.
Rejoice in hope, endure in affliction, persevere in prayer.
Contribute to the needs of the holy ones, exercise hospitality.
Bless those who persecute you, bless and do not curse them.
Rejoice with those who rejoice, weep with those who weep.
Have the same regard for one another;
Do not be haughty but associate with the lowly;
Do not be wise in your own estimation.
Do not repay anyone evil for evil;
be concerned for what is noble in the sight of all.
Live at peace with all.
Beloved, do not look for revenge.
Rather, if your enemy is hungry, feed them;
if they are thirsty, give them something to drink;
for by so doing you will heap burning coals upon their head.
Do not be conquered by evil but conquer evil with good.

–Romans 12: 9-21

Help the Church to Return
to the Nonviolence of Jesus

Dear God,

Thank you for the Church, for all the churches,
for the global Christian community.
Thank you for giving us sisters and brothers
who also want to follow the nonviolent Jesus
on the road to your peace.
Thank you for the blessings of communion,
the Gospels, our priests and ministers,
the sacraments, our traditions,
and all the blessings you give to communities of Jesus.

Dear God,
please help your Church,
all your churches,
to renounce the just war theory
and the myth of redemptive violence.
Return us to the nonviolence of Jesus,
to the Sermon on the Mount and Jesus' call
for universal love, universal compassion,
and universal peace.

We repent for centuries of betraying Jesus.
We are sorry for supporting war, killing enemies,
holding people as slaves, burning women at the stake,
putting down the marginalized, serving the rich,
blessing nuclear weapons, and invoking your name
on every side in every war since the days
of the early Church.

We repent.
We are sorry.
We want to change.

We want to return to the nonviolence of Jesus.
Help us to live as he lived,
practice peace as he practiced it,
resist injustice as he did,
suffer and die nonviolently as he did,
and share in the new life of resurrection peace
as he now does.

Dear God,
the Church still supports violence,
racism, sexism, war, weapons,
greed, money, and environmental destruction.
We focus on money, success, power, and fame,
instead of prayer, humility, loving kindness,
and nonviolence.
We want to change, but we don't know how.

Give us the gift of a global conversion
to the Sermon on the Mount,
to the nonviolence of Jesus,
that we might reflect the peace and compassion
of Jesus himself in these terrible times,
that we might be your instruments of peace,
that he might rejoice in our fidelity.

Thank you for hearing our prayer.
Amen.

Part Ten:

For the Coming of God's Reign of Peace and Nonviolence

———○———

A king is not saved by a mighty army,
nor a warrior delivered by great strength.
Useless is the horse for safety;
Its great strength, no sure escape.
But the lord's eyes are upon the reverent,
upon those who hope for God's gracious help.
Delivering them from death, keeping them alive . . . .
Our soul waits for the God of peace,
who is our help and shield.
For in God our hearts rejoice,
in your holy name we trust.
May your kindness, God of peace, be upon us;
We have put our hope in you.

–Psalm 33: 16-22

Give Us the Grace to Do Your Will of Peace, Love, and Nonviolence, to Welcome Your Reign of Peace, Love, and Nonviolence Here on Earth

Dear God,

The key prayer of Jesus is simple and to the point:
"Your kingdom come, your will be done,
on earth as it is in heaven."

Dear God, your kingdom, your realm,
is a new world of nonviolence, love, and peace;
your will is for the coming of that new world
of nonviolence, love, and peace.

We beg you: please give us your kingdom
of nonviolence, love, and peace.
Please help us to turn from doing our own will
to doing your will,
to spend our lives practicing, teaching, and organizing
peace, love, and nonviolence.

We want the coming of your reign
of peace and nonviolence on earth,
but we do not know what to do, how to help.
We are stuck in mindless violence, selfishness, and war.
We barely know you.
We hardly believe.

Yet your reign, your will, are for our own good.
You want only good for us.
You want us to live nonviolently
toward ourselves and one another.
You want us to end war, poverty,
injustice, and destruction,
that we might welcome your reign of peace on earth.
This is your will.

May it be our will, too.

Give us a new grace to do your will
of peace, love, and nonviolence,
and so to welcome your reign
of peace, love, and nonviolence
concretely here on earth.

In Jesus' name,
Amen.

Make Us Citizens of Your Reign

Dear God,

Forgive us.
Despite everything the nonviolent Jesus taught,
we are stuck in nationalism.
That means we are stuck in idolatry.

We have been raised to worship the idols
of money, career, bank accounts, guns,
war, even weapons of mass destruction.
We are trained individualists,
taught to ignore the suffering masses around the world,
to focus only on ourselves.
We have been bred with an innate sense of entitlement—
the world is ours, the money and resources are ours,
everything should come our way, we are first.

We are far from your kingdom of nonviolence,
your reign of peace and love.
We have pledged allegiance to the wrong realm.

In your mercy, help us to reclaim our true citizenship
in your kingdom of nonviolence,
your reign of peace and love.

Help us to live every minute as if we are truly citizens
of your kingdom of nonviolence,
your reign of peace and love.

Give us the grace to practice your politics,
the politics of universal peace, love, and nonviolence.

From now on, dear God, we are citizens
of your kingdom of nonviolence,
citizens of your realm of universal peace and love.
From now on, we live in your reign,
in your presence, in your will.

Amen.

Part Eleven:

For Life in the
Holy Spirit of Peace

May God grant you in accord with the riches of his glory
to be strengthened with power through God's Spirit
in the inner self, and that Christ may dwell
in your hearts through faith;
that you, rooted and grounded in love,
may have strength to comprehend with all the holy ones,
what is the breadth and length and height and depth,
and to know the love of Christ that surpasses knowledge,
so that you may be filled with all the fullness of God.

–Ephesians 3:16-19

May the God of peace give you peace
at all times and in every way.

–2 Thessalonians 3:16

Give Us the Holy Spirit of the Nonviolent Jesus That We Might Live in His Peace, Love, and Nonviolence from Now On

Dear God,

Please give us the Holy Spirit of the nonviolent Jesus,
that we might live fully in his Holy Spirit
from now on, from this day until our last.

His Holy Spirit is the spirit
of love, compassion, nonviolence, and peace.
We need his Holy Spirit.
You want us to live in his Holy Spirit.
These are the days of the Holy Spirit.
We are so blessed to live fully in his Holy Spirit.
You would give us his Spirit simply for the asking.

But dear God, have mercy on us.
We are stuck in the unholy spirit
of violence, hatred, narcissism,
greed, war, and destruction.
We think only of ourselves.
We are blind.
We don't know our left hand from our right.
We want to be rich, successful, powerful, and honored.
We do not want to live in your Holy Spirit
of humility, kindness, vulnerability,
gentleness, nonviolence, and love.
We want the unholy spirit of pride, honor,
domination, power, violence, and hatred.

Dear God, we need your Holy Spirit
now more than ever.
By giving in to the demons of violence,
we suffer and die in a world of permanent war,
systemic injustice, racism, sexism, and violence,
all under the possibility of nuclear war

and catastrophic climate change.
If we do not choose your Holy Spirit of nonviolence,
we will destroy ourselves with total global violence.

We need your Holy Spirit
of peace, love, and nonviolence.
Give it to us, give it to me, now and forever.

Your Holy Spirit of peace, love,
and nonviolence is our only hope.
No, we do not deserve it.
But you love us.
You are the living God
of peace, love, and nonviolence.

Give us your Holy Spirit,
that we might live in the Holy Spirit
of the nonviolent Jesus from now on,
that we might spread your Holy Spirit
of peace, love, and nonviolence far and wide,
that we might become who you created us to be,
your beloved sons and daughters,
your holy peacemakers.

Thank you.
Amen.

Part Twelve:

For Humanity's Conversion to Total Nonviolence

Then the wolf shall be a guest of the lamb,
and the leopard shall lie down with the kid;
the calf and the young lion shall browse together,
with a little child to guide them.
The cow and the bear shall be neighbors,
together their young shall rest;
the lion shall eat hay like the ox.
The baby shall play by the cobra's den,
and the child lay his hand on the adder's lair.
There shall be no harm or ruin on all my holy mountain;
for the earth shall be filled
with knowledge of the God of peace.

–Isaiah 11:6-9

Then I saw a new heaven and a new earth . . . .
I heard a loud voice from the throne saying,
"Behold, God's dwelling is with the human race.
God will dwell with them and
they will be God's people and
God will always be with them.
God will wipe every tear from their eyes,
and there shall be no more death or mourning,
wailing or pain, for the old order has passed away.

–Revelation 21:1-4

Please Convert the Entire Human Race to Jesus' Way of Total Nonviolence

Dear God,

In the end, there is only one prayer:
please convert the entire human race
to Jesus' way of total nonviolence.

That is our only hope.
This is Jesus' daily prayer.
This is the will of the Holy Spirit.
This is your deepest desire.
Convert us all to the Way, the Truth, and the Life
of active, loving nonviolence.

Help us turn to you, our Higher Power;
to renounce violence;
to make amends for our long history of violence;
and to become sober people of nonviolence,
that from now on, we might live
within the boundaries of nonviolence—
and do no harm to anyone ever again.
Instead, may we love, serve, and make peace
with all our sisters and brothers
around the world
from now on.

Give us a new grace:
may we never again support the taking
of a single human life,
no matter what the cause,
no matter what we are told.

May we never harm or kill another person,
threaten entire peoples, wage war,
or terrify the world with the possibility of nuclear
annihilation.

May we beat our swords, guns, and bombs
into plowshares of peace, and never study war again.

May we abolish war, guns, and nuclear weapons,
and learn by heart your methodology
of nonviolent conflict resolution, universal love,
and Gospel peacemaking.

Help us to study peace and build grassroots movements
of disarmament, justice, and nonviolence.
Help us to institutionalize nonviolent conflict resolution
locally, nationally, and globally
and to create new structures for new cultures
of peace and nonviolence.

Our future is a future of peace and nonviolence.
Help us to envision that new future,
that new world, that new hope.
Give us the grace to do our part to make
that vision of peace come true.

Help me to be converted to your way of nonviolence.
Give every human being the grace
to be converted to your way of nonviolence.
Bless us that we might all follow
the nonviolent Jesus on the path of peace
and welcome his resurrection gift of peace
in our hearts and on earth.

Make your peace a true reality here and now
for every human being, every creature,
and Mother Earth, from now on.
Give us your reign of peace and nonviolence
on earth as it is in heaven.

Make us as nonviolent as Jesus.
Amen.

About the Author

Rev. John Dear is an internationally recognized voice and leader for peace and nonviolence. A priest, activist and author, he served for years as the director of the Fellowship of Reconciliation, the largest interfaith peace organization in the US. After September 11, 2001, he was a Red Cross coordinator of chaplains at the Family Assistance Center in New York, and counseled thousands of relatives and rescue workers. John has traveled the war zones of the world, been arrested some 80 times for peace, led Nobel Peace prize winners to Iraq, recently visited Afghanistan, given thousands of lectures on peace across the US, and served as a pastor of several churches in New Mexico. He arranged on many occasions for Mother Teresa to speak to various governors to stop an impending execution, and recently helped draft Pope Francis' January 1, 2017 World Day of Peace message on nonviolence. He is a co-founder of Campaign Nonviolence and the Nonviolent Cities Project, and is on the staff of Pace e Bene.

He is the author of thirty-six books, including: *The Nonviolent Life; They Will Inherit the Earth; Walking the Way; The Beatitudes of Peace; Thomas Merton Peacemaker; A Persistent Peace; Transfiguration; You Will Be My Witnesses; Living Peace; The Questions of Jesus; The God of Peace; Jesus the Rebel; Peace Behind Bars; Lazarus Come Forth!* and *Disarming the Heart.* He has been nominated many times for the Nobel Peace Prize, including by Archbishop Desmond Tutu and Sen. Barbara Mikulski. He works for CampaignNonviolence.org, is a priest of the Diocese of Monterey, CA, and lives in New Mexico.

JohnDear.org

About Pace e Bene/Campaign Nonviolence

Pace e Bene is a nearly thirty-year-old peace organization, inspired by the Franciscans, to teach and promote active nonviolence. Today, Pace e Bene organizes Campaign Nonviolence, a national week of action every September, which in 2017 inspired over 1000 actions across the USA in every state, against racism, poverty, war, and environmental destruction and for the coming of a new culture of peace and nonviolence.

Pace e Bene also organizes the Nonviolent Cities project, to get local communities to envision and transform their community into a nonviolent city. It holds nonviolence trainings, workshops, and lectures; publishes workbooks and books on active nonviolence; and uses social media to promote nonviolence around the world.

For further information, visit Paceebene.org, email: info@paceebene.org, call: 510-268-8765.

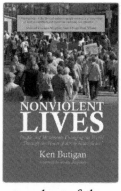